Return to the High Country

Return to the High Country

New Tales of a High Sierra Pack Cook

Irene Kritz

aventine press

Published by Aventine Press
55 East Emerson St.
Chula Vista CA, 91911
www.aventinepress.com

ISBN: 978-1-59330-982-4

Library of Congress Control Number: 2020916630
Library of Congress Cataloging-in-Publication Data
Return to the High Country/ Irene Kritz

Printed in the United States of America

Contents

Once Upon An Owens Valley Day…   7

First Time As A Real Live Packer   11

Pack Mules From The Twenty Mule Team   15

Packing With Ty And Other Stuff From Reds Meadows   21

Art The Wonder Horse   27

Books?   33

Love In The High Lonesome   37

Adventures With One Giant Mule   41

First Mustang Trip In The Pizona   49

No Danged Horses   55

Ridin' Fence At The Pool Field   61

Uh, No, I Don't Speak Japanese. Does It Matter?   67

Forest Fire   77

Guess Who I Met On The Trail   83

Sometimes A Hero…   93

Blizzard On Mono Pass   97

Mountain Dogs   101

Once Upon A Magic Place   107

The Long, Long Trip   115

Sage Flats, Monache, And Beyond   131

ONCE UPON AN OWENS VALLEY DAY…

The "Lone Pine Chamber Lady" asked Tyler the Packer to write a brief story about how much fun it was to take a pack trip in the High Sierra. Somehow the fact that he had over a hundred head of horses and mules to get ready for the summer and the fact I had once written a book about packing led to the tentative agreement that I would write this thing. Being as I can no longer find my butt with both hands and a map, I promptly forgot. Now that it has been called to my attention, I guess I should get busy.

First off, there are a lot of fun things to be done up in the high lonesome. Of course, a whole lot of them aren't fit to be mentioned in this little writing. You know, like the time we caught two forest rangers in the middle of a trail, displaying no clothes and a lot of affection. That was pretty darn funny, but I suppose I should have left it out.

Anyhow, after a day on the trail watching the most beautiful country in the world move past your mule's ears, you spend the afternoon fishing, hiking, swimming, birding, wading through wildflowers or just reading in the shade of a majestic pine. Then at five it's cocktail hour and if you can beat the loose mules to the table you might enjoy relaxing with snacks and drinks. Then everyone enjoys a hearty meal cooked over a fire and then adjourns to the campfire to be entertained by whatever that evening may offer. I remember one trip I took when the guests were so darn funny that I laughed for seven days straight and when I finally returned to the pack station, I was still laughing so hard that I fell out of the van when we got there.

Campfire entertainment varies widely. Sometimes it's terrible, like if you have a dude who likes to read aloud from "Place Names in the High Sierra." Wow, boring! Much better was last summer when we had the privilege of listening to a tall, handsome Aussie packer recite the famous Aussie poem, "The Man from Snowy River." I used to have a boss who beside being one of the greatest packers of all time also could play guitar and sing better than any famous country star that I ever heard. On the trail you almost always have someone who plays harmonica or guitar or sings. Many also write their own songs and you get to be the first to hear their most recent piece of music. You run across people who make music, recite cowboy poetry, tell true stories, tell jokes, and sometimes just lie outright.

Sometimes you also get to run across the cowboy sense of humor, which to say the least is a little cruel around the edges. Typically, that is like when someone looks at what's left of your arm after a rough bronc has stomped it into the mud and says, "Heck, it's a long way from you heart. Let's get back to work." Once I had three days of riding where I just couldn't get comfortable on that old dude horse. Seems as how the wrangler who was saddling up my horse each morning thought it would be fun to readjust my stirrups every day so they were always a few inches different in length. Jerk! Once the boss chewed us out for making lunch sandwiches that were too plain. He ended up by warning us there better be onion in his lunch the next day. Didn't seem real pleased when his lunch sack that day held nothing but one big, old onion.

On a different trip with another boss with a warped sense of humor, we had a random group of guests who didn't know each other. The boss picked out two big young guys as his victims. The first night he took one of them aside and pointing to the other one told him that he was an ex-convict with a bad temper and that he should steer clear of him especially if he offered him a drink. The following night he delivered the same warning to the second guy about the first one. Then he just sat back for the rest of the trip watching these two guys tiptoe around each other.

One day we were resting on a layover day at Crabtree meadows while some of the packers were pulling cache from the last camp. One packer leading his string across the meadow was accosted by one of those lady guests who have read one too many western romance novels.

Batting her eyelashes and holding up a bedraggled yellow monkey-flower in her hand, she stepped in front of his horse and simpered "Oh, Mr. Packer, you know so much about the wilderness, can you tell me what this is?" Pulling up his horse, the packer politely removed his hat and said, "Why, yes, Ma'm. Up here in the high lonesome, we call that a flower." And replacing his hat, he nodded to her and rode on.

Other times I burned a round pan of brownies and we used it to play Frisbee on the meadow. It lasted several days and when it wore out, we missed it so much that we made a soccer ball out of scrap paper and duct tape to replace it. There's lots more I could mention, but instead, why don't you join us up there sometime?

FIRST TIME AS A REAL LIVE PACKER

When I first wandered into a job with Mt Whitney Pack Trains, I started out as a station cook, then a camp cook, then a trail cook, and eventually added guide, wrangler, and packer. On my second day there the boss, Tommy Jefferson, called the new female employees together and rather forcefully explained that since we were women, none (and he meant NONE) of us would ever be packers. Therefore, he didn't want to see any of us messing around with the mules, fooling around with the pack equipment (or the packer's equipment!) or anything else that wasn't officially women's work. Just as I was working my way up to being pretty ticked off, he stopped all us cold by adding that anyone who broke this rule would be fired, then and there.

Over the next few years, us horsey girls had to be satisfied with kitchen work, trail cooking, and day rides. Along the way I looked and listened real careful as the experienced packers shared their wisdom with the new guys. On days when there were no men around the station, sometimes we would hang a packsaddle and bags on the hitchrail and practice throwing a diamond. I wasn't lookin' to be a packer, especially since lifting those 75-pound side loads on a 16 hand mule was pretty close to being beyond me. But over the years it had become obvious to me that emergencies were everyday occurrences in this business, and it might be a real good idea to be able to get out of the back country on your own.

Late in my second summer at MWPT, we hit that point where practically everyone and everything was on the trail in the back country.

I had just come out from a trip and was just about the only crewmember at the station. Tommy was there but he was just about to hit the road. He called me aside and told me that he had a small spot trip to go to Mirror Lake and that he wanted me to take it. I objected that surely he must realize that I didn't know how to pack. He assured me that he knew that I could pack and that I better get busy.

It should have been a cinch, but of course it wasn't. Mirror Lake was only three or four miles up the Whitney trail, all before the high, dangerous part of the trail. I only had one load of stuff to deliver to some hikers there. Shoulda been easy, but... First off, we were out of mules, so I would have to pack a saddle horse that wasn't used to being packed. Second, though I was only packing 90 pounds of stuff, it was fastened onto 3 separate backpack frames. I had strict instructions not to rearrange any of the packs and the packs were 20, 30, and 40 pounds. You tell me how you make a balanced load out of that. Well I tried my best and we started off up the trail.

Duke, the saddle horse, wasn't real pleased with his new job. I kept a close eye on his load, but by the time we were two miles along, I could see that his load was starting to slip. We were on a steep side hill not too far below Lone Pine Lake. It was just dirt, brush and pine trees, so I decided it looked like I could stop and repack right in the trail. I pulled the packs off and added some rocks to the pack bag on what appeared to be the lighter side. A fair number of hikers had come down the trail, but they were kind enough to stop and wait for me to finish. The side loads appeared to be pretty well matched so I lifted the third pack up on top of the pack saddle. Then my foot slipped on the pine needles and I lost my hold on the top pack. The packframe slipped back and dug in the horse's back right above his kidneys. Allowing as how that pretty much hurt, old Duke tried to duck away, lost his balance and tumbled off the trail. He fell and rolled twice ending up upside down with his feet in the air and his pack saddle wedged against three small pine trees. He didn't appear to be hurt, just stuck.

So now all I had to do was pick up the scattered load, get the rest of the load off the pack saddle, and then unfasten the saddle so that it would come off and let Duke roll on over and onto his feet. By this time, we had quite an audience standing on the trail watching our little disaster. With Duke off the trail they could have all gone on, but I guess we were the afternoon's entertainment. Luckily Duke wasn't struggling and I managed to remove the rest of the load pretty easily. I could see that freeing the pack saddle was going to be the hard part. The cinch was fastened with a quick-release knot, but to reach that knot I would have to crawl in under the horse on the downhill side. I got hold of the knot and worked my legs into a position where I could jump free as soon as the horse started to roll. So, I jerked hard on the latigo, everything started to move and I jumped for my life.

As I scrambled clear of 1100 pounds of rolling horse, I felt a hoof brush across my head. I could hear one of the hikers screaming, "She's dead! She's dead! I saw the horse roll over her! She's dead!" I hollered back at her to shut up before she scared the stock. And besides I was pretty sure I wasn't dead.

It took about half an hour to get everybody and everything back up on the trail and repacked. Duke didn't seem much the worse for wear, so we went on up the trail. The rest of the trail passed Lone Pine Lake isolated down in a pristine pocket, wound around Outpost Camp with its thundering waterfall, and climbed on up to Mirror Lake. That ride would normally have been a real pleasure, but I was mostly too wore out to care.

At Mirror Lake I found my hikers and delivered the load. I dutifully explained that we had had a wreck and asked them to check their stuff for damage. The father of this family group discovered that one of his camera lenses was missing from an outside pocket of his pack. His description of the value of the lens was real horrifying to a person who was making a salary of $5.00 a day. I really couldn't make it right, but I assured him that I would search the wreck site on my way out. I hung my head and rode out listening to him muttering that I had ruined his entire trip.

By the time I reached the area below Lone Pine Lake where the wreck had taken place it was close on to dark and just starting to rain. I searched the entire area with no luck. Eventually I crawled on hands and knees through the rain-wet pine needles. Still no luck. Giving it up to the dark, I muttered some off-color word, kicked a rock and started to stomp back to my horse. The small rock rolled over revealing a tiny pocket in the pine needles which just happened to hold a camera lens in a leather case.

I grabbed up the lens, jumped on my horse, and giggled most of the way back in the rain. Several days later the lens owner came by the station. All proud of having found it, I presented him with the little treasure safe in its leather case. He allowed as how I had still ruined his entire trip. He said that I was the worst packer that ever lived and that he was going to write to my boss and get me fired. I should have been pretty depressed, but after this trip I had pretty much decided that I never wanted to be a packer anyway.

PACK MULES FROM THE TWENTY MULE TEAM

When you gather around the campfire to sing and joke and tell stories, sometimes the best stories that drift into your mind are not your own little wilderness adventures, but tales you heard from the old timers long, long ago. This story is made up of quite a few such memories. As you all know, mules were used to haul huge loads of borax out of Death Valley in the days before there were paved roads and trucks doing the job. You have all seen pictures of the big teams of twenty mules hauling two huge ore wagons and a water wagon that was almost as big. Any such a rig that was working later than 1930 was a reenactment, or for a celebration, or a parade, or for a movie or TV film. Since good mules and great mule men were getting pretty rare by then, most of the mules and their handlers were working the rest of the year for pack trains in the sierras.

When I first came to work for Mt Whitney Pack Trains in 1964, some of the guys pointed out three mules in the stock pen and proudly stated that the were the last of "the" twenty mule team. At first I didn't get it being as it had been more than forty years since such teams worked the road from Death Valley to Mojave. It seemed that in 1949 Death Valley staged a centennial celebration. The high point of that event included the recreation of a twenty-mule team and its wagons. They apparently borrowed twenty matched black mules from Mt Whitney Pack Trains and broke them to drive. Then to get to Death Valley for the ceremonies, they drove the mules and wagons there from Lone Pine. That's 100 miles of desert and rugged mountains, just like the old days. Those big rigs moved at about two miles an hour when things were going well and it took them ten days to get from Lone Pine to Death Valley. I don't know all the trainers and drivers, but it seems to me the names that came up were Bruce Morgan (owner of MWPT), Russ Spainhower (owner of Anchor Ranch), and Pete Olivas (local boy, movie extra, and all around great storyteller).

The mules that were pointed out to me were all big, black, and pretty old. They were Ike, Dina, and Fred. On the team Ike was a wheel mule, Dina was a point mule, and Fred was a lead mule. Dina, as a point mule was one of the second or third pairs in front of the wagon. Her job was to get that huge outfit around corners. On a corner all the other teams would swing around the corner while the wheelers and pointers pulled the wagon straight ahead. To do this the outside point mule of each pair would jump the center chain so they could keep pulling the wagons straight ahead. The wheel mules were on a singletree and held the wagon straight. When the other 16 mules were past the turn, the point mules and wheelers would bring the wagons around. To do that the pointers would of course have to jump back over the center chain. Even though Dina was talented enough to be a point mule, at Whitney she was just another pack mule. The only actual memory I have of her was when she was turned out at Big Whitney Meadow on a Livermore trip and she got caught in a bog. She was in so deep that it took two guys with shovels a long time to dig her out. Dina Livermore, wife of the leader of that trip, was hysterical until they got the mule safely out. I think the mule was her namesake and she was pretty attached to her. Anyway, they saved the mule and everything turned out fine.

Fred was a lead mule when he was with the twenty-mule team. That means that he was in the front and that the single long rein went all the way from the driver on the wheel mule up to him in the lead. He was the mule that got the directions and led all the other mules. By the time I met him at MWPT he was old and tired and had been demoted to lunch mule. In those days we didn't make sack lunches for the guests. With larger groups of riders, we would take one old, quiet mule and pack him with all the lunch supplies for that day plus coffee pots, a grate, firewood, a table and all the needed utensils. At noon we would stop off the trail, unpack the mule, build a campfire to make coffee and tea and put out all the makings for lunch. We would spend at least an hour at lunch so that the mule strings had time to pass us. That way the strings could get to camp far enough ahead of us to be unpacked and out of camp by the time the guests arrived. Fred was a great mule and I got to lead him some of the time. He was kind and gentle and careful. He gave me my first impression of what a pack mule was like. Later I learned that he was the exception rather than the rule. But, boy, did I like that old mule.

Then there was Ike, named after Ike Livermore, one of the owners of Mt Whitney Pack Trains. Ike was the wheel mule. Since wheelers often carried a rider and were the only animals that had to deal with the wagon tongue, they tended to be bigger and more stout than most of the other mules in the team. This really helped when they were the ones along with the point mules who had to pull everything while the other mules made the corner. When I say everything, I mean the whole shebang, around 30 tons of wagons, borax, and equipment. After the centennial finished up in Death Valley, they went to numerous other events. But eventually the mules returned to working as pack mules in the sierras. Within the next few years Ike became locally famous as the "compressor mule." Now that's another long story, but it seems I can't resist telling it. Sometime around 1950 the Forest Service decided that they had to do something about the Whitney trail. You see when the trail was first built, the section from Trail Camp (12,000 ft) and Trail Crest (13,000 ft) was built straight up a col. At first glance it seemed the most obvious way. But in practice it was a slot that led straight up between two cliffs and was in just the right place to make sure that the snow it held never, ever melted. The new plan involved blasting a series of 97 short switchbacks straight up the face of the cliff to the left of the col. To do this you needed a compressor to drill holes for the explosives. Such a compressor would weigh about 450 pounds and there was no way to haul it to the pad at the 12,000-foot level except by pack mule. Most pack loads vary from 150 to 200 pounds. A big mule can carry 300 pounds if they have to, but not for long and not in real steep country.

So, the Whitney trail from the pack station at Whitney Portals to the compressor pad above Trail Camp is a rocky 8 mile pull with a rise of 4000 feet in elevation. But Ike did it and according to several of the old timers, this is how he did it. First, they got him in condition. Since there is no such thing as a mule gym, they took him on all the trips for a couple of months before the big haul. To condition him without wearing him down, he didn't carry any loads during that time. They designed the equipment with an aparejo saddle for Ike. This is a metal framework resting on two leather pads stuffed with grass. This raises the load above the animal's withers. Then they took a second mule loaded with an A frame. So, Ike started off up the trail with 450 pounds of steel balanced high above his back. He kept going until his packer spotted any sign of fatigue. Then they would stop and unpack the A frame from the second mule. This was a frame much like those used to raise engines out of cars, only larger. They would set it up around Ike and lift the compressor into the air above him, where it stayed while he rested. When Ike was ready, they would reverse the procedure and continue on up the trail. Of course, they needed to complete this in a single day and as I understand it, they did just that. After that Ike was famous as a twenty-mule team wheeler and as the Whitney Trail compressor mule.

Well, that's pretty much the story of Mt. Whitney Pack Trains and the Twenty Mule Team mules. In the fifty-some years since then there have been other twenty mule teams. About 20 years ago Bobby Tanner of Reds Meadows Pack Station trained and drove a twenty-mule team made up of red mules from the outfit. Bobby drove them in a lot of parades and shows such as Mule Days, the Rose Parade and other big mule events. I never got to know those animals except for Bobby's wheel mule, Star. White face markings are pretty rare on mules, so I recognized Star when he worked as a saddle mule on some trips I worked for Reds.

The best postscript to this is that in 2016, Bobby trained a new team of black mules and with some really talented help built new exact replicas of the borax wagons, water tanker and harnesses. They introduced the new outfit to the public at the Rose Parade. It was outstanding and what a thrill to watch the point mules jump the chain to make the turn onto Colorado Blvd. Sent shivers up my back to see it.

You know, on July 4th, 2017, it was a great surprise and pleasure to encounter a video of that outfit together with a lot of Eastern Sierra folks including the Tanners and the Roessers parked on the street in Washington, DC. It was big wagons, 20 mules, and the Washington Monument in the background. Wow, really just wow.

FYI, if you want to see pictures of the 1949 outfit going to Death Valley, go to the Owens Valley History website and find the part about Bruce Morgan and the Twenty Mule Team. It has a good shot of Ike working as the wheel mule.

PACKING WITH TY AND OTHER STUFF
FROM REDS MEADOWS

I tell a lot of these stories around the campfire being as how entertaining the guests is part of my job. As time goes by, they get pretty organized and even kinda polished. Then there are the other kind of stories that just sorta happen when you are working around camp at jobs that require time but very little concentration. These stories just flow from your memory with very little planning or organization. Real writers call these something like "train of consciousness." Bullshitters like me just call them running off at the mouth. Seems kinda obvious that this is gonna be one of those stories.

Getting my first trip with Reds Meadows Pack was just a touch difficult. Reds was a big outfit running over 200 head of stock out of two different pack stations; Reds Meadows and Agnew. I was spending my summers at Carroll Creek about 10 miles out of Lone Pine. The rest of the year I worked as a teacher in Lone Pine. At Carroll Creek we had about 20 head of horses, no phone, no electricity, and a do-it-yourself water system. My first husband, Walt, spent most of his time fighting fires for the forest service. He was helitack foreman for the Mt Whitney District of the Inyo National Forest. He could be called out at a moment's notice for fires as far away as Montana and be gone for as long as three weeks at a time.

Eventually Walt was promoted to Fire Management Officer for the district. This meant he was gone much less often. We also had gained some friends who would care for our animals if we were both gone at the same time. I had reached the point where I desperately missed summer packing in the mountains. My new situation meant it would probably be okay to be gone for a week at a time, maybe two or three times a summer. But not being able to sign on for a whole summer would likely make it pretty hard to get a job. Mt Whitney Pack Trains had gone under and many of the packers that I knew had moved on.

Then one day I had a horse that required vet attention, so I took her to Bishop Vet Hospital where the vets are an outstanding group of cattle ranchers, packers, horsemen, and mule men. While Dr. Tom Talbot was working on the horse, we got to BS-ing about the livestock business in this area. Tom asked me if I was still working packing in the back country. I allowed as how my home situation only let me to be gone for a week or so at a time. Therefore, I was currently unemployed in the packing business where cooks and packers regularly signed on for full time from June through September. Tom thought for a bit then told me that he had recently spoken to several pack owners who were looking for trail cooks to fill in during their busiest times of the season. In fact, Tom said that just the day before he had spoken to Bob Tanner, owner of Reds Meadows, who was apparently desperate for an extra cook.

Tom made the suggestion that I contact Bob and if this trip worked out, I could start a business where I contracted out to cook for various outfits when they were short of a cook and their schedule fit mine. Well, this struck me as a fine idea, a chance to get back into the high country for at least part of each summer. Of course, it all hinged on the success or failure of this first trip for Tanner.

Living at Carroll Creek meant that I had no phone service except the battery-run, mountain line to Monache Meadows. The nearest thing I had to regular phone service was an answering service with the Dow Villa Hotel in Lone Pine. Using that phone, I called Reds Meadows to see if they might have a job for an itinerant trail cook. The phone was answered by the boss's wife, Jean Tanner. She seemed shocked by my inquiry and informed me that Reds Meadows had all the hands they needed. Also, that it was the best outfit in the Sierras and whoever had implied they needed more help was just trying to make trouble. She then "kindly" offered to take my number in case they ever needed someone. By then I was pretty pissed off and almost didn't give her my number.

Fortunately, I did end up leaving my number and 24 hours later when I checked my calls at the Dow there was a message from Bob saying that I was hired and needed to be at Reds the next day. Guess he had left Jean out of the loop and she hadn't known he was looking for help.

So, the next day I was in the big canyon back of Mammoth Mountain at Reds Meadows Pack Trains. It looked to be quite a challenge. I had the rest of the afternoon and that night to put together the lists, food, and equipment for a four-day trip for six guests. Bob told me that when I got done, I could sleep on the ground back of the store. He was thoughtful enough to mention that I should stay away from the dumpsters as there were three large bears that came there every night. As it turned out I had so much to do that night that I never got to sleep at all, let alone to sleep with the bears.

The next day Bob and the guests had some kind of discussion that resulted in changing the itinerary of the whole trip. We had to truck all the horses, mules, tack, camp equipment, and food seven miles to Agnew Meadows, the new starting point for our trip. We finally put our guest hikers on the trail ahead of us around 11 AM. It was close to noon when the stock, strings, and crew hit the trail. Our ride was to Clark Lakes, a medium length move up toward the headwaters of the San Joaquin River.

One of my truly vivid memories of pack cooking in the Sierras was that night at Clark Lakes. Since we'd made a late start, it was well after dark by the time I started getting ready to cook dinner. The wind was howling and starting a cook fire wasn't easy. The duff and kindling blew away while I tried to light it. Every time I lit a match, it blew out before I could get it to the wood. I don't know actually how long it took to get that fire started but I do know it took more than fifty of those big wooden kitchen matches. During this entire struggle I kept asking myself, over and over, why I was back in the high lonesome working at a job that had a lot in common with beating your head on a rock.

Reds Meadows had their cooks work off a standardized menu. It wasn't exactly the best menu I ever worked with. It was great the first night with steaks, baked potatoes, salad, garlic bread, and strawberry shortcake. The second night was okay with pre-cooked roast reheated with gravy, instant mashed potatoes, etc. By the third night it was pretty mediocre and was basically canned stew. Then it went downhill to stuff like tuna surprise. Nothing pissed me off more than having to serve meals than I couldn't be proud of. So, before I left on this trip, I stocked up on some stuff I swiped out of the store and kitchen at Reds and made some radical changes in our menu. My swelled head wants to think that this turned out so well that my guests sent Bob a letter that made the crew sound like we could walk on water. But my cooking was only part of it. The rest of what made this trip great was my new packer, Tyrone Robert Atwater III.

Ty was what could be described as a kick in the pants to work with. He knew the country and was good with stock. He treated the guests kindly. He carried his share of the workload and then some. But best of all was his story telling. Actually, he turned out to be the one who had told the Reds Meadows crew about the time I almost knifed Ted back at Mount Whitney. Of course, he had padded the story up until it sounded like I had killed poor old Ted. No wonder the rest of the Reds crew gave me a wide berth that first summer.

Ty had a way with words. I remember the year that he quit Reds to go and pack in the Grand Tetons. We have all seen magnificent pictures of those beautiful mountains and Ty was just thrilled to death to be headed there. What most people don't realize is that the Tetons are a narrow ridge that always seemed to me like a cardboard cut-out of a mountain range.

You ride in one side, top out, and are on your way out the other side. In less than a month, Ty was back working at Reds and telling us stories about roping and packing a yearling elk. Finally, I broke down and asked why he didn't stay in the Tetons. He simply said, "I thought I would like the Tetons, but there ain't no mountains in them mountains."

Another of my favorite Ty stories happened several years later when we were hauling a group of old ladies up the high trail above Agnew. We stopped at an overlook across from Shadow Lake. While our fairly senior group of guests rested their horses, Ty launched into a lengthy geological explanation of the creation of the canyons across from us. Ty explained how the last ice age, of about 10,000 years ago, had produced glaciers that carved out the steep walls of the canyon below us. In a ringing voice he described how the glacial ice had rolled over the jagged granite hills across from us leaving smooth, rounded hills scraped clean of all jagged edges and shining with glacial polish. Then pointing to the 200-year-old pines growing in the pockets among those hills, he confided to his listeners that the thing that surprised him the most was that the glaciers had left all those trees standing. As he turned and led the group on up the trail, he glanced back throwing me a wicked grin over his shoulder. Riding drag behind our guests, I listened to them wondering in amazement at how the pines had survived the glacial onslaught. And I rode up the trail behind them with both hands pressed tight on my mouth to hold in the laughter.

Now returning to that first trip with Reds, after that hard night at Clark Lakes we made a short move to the little side canyon just below the outlet of Thousand Island Lake which is the beginning of the San Joaquin River. Our next little camp brings back many memories. That was the time in history when Sky Lab was falling out of the sky. Every night it would pass directly overhead getting bigger and brighter as it got lower with each pass. Around the campfire much of the talk concerned what were the odds that it would eventually land in our laps. As we all know it eventually landed in Australia, but it was fun while it lasted.

The guests on this trip were very concerned with the quality of food that came out of our camp kitchen. They had brought some really good vittles to add to our kitchen supplies including fresh-squeezed orange juice, avocados, fresh fruit and some very nice wines. In light of this I was incredibly embarrassed by the fact that I was supposed to feed them Dinty Moore canned stew for the third dinner. So, from the beginning I began plotting and hoarding food so that I could change the menu. So I swiped some steak from the first night and some roast from the second night, took half of the potatoes meant for baking, loaded up on veggies from the Reds kitchen before we left and we ended up with a dinner made up of tossed green salad, homemade beef stew, freshly baked biscuits, and peach cobbler. Everyone was pleased, especially Ty who knew what the meal was supposed to be.

That same night after dinner, I learned a few things I hadn't known about wines. The guests had saved a very nice Chateau Nuff de Pape '57 for our last night. That is a Rhone wine and I learned that Rhones for some reason hold up well to bouncing down the trail on top of a mule. Around the fire that night we had a second wine that was a host gift from the ranger we had invited to dinner. This nice gift from the ranger fell into a different class of wines from the Rhone. It was in a glass jug with a plain lick-on label which was rubber stamped with the words "Red Wine." Funny that as the evening wore on and the bottles of wine and some other various types of alcoholic beverages circled the campfire, we all eventually reached the stage where no one could tell the fine wine from the jug wine. Guess no one is much of a wine expert once he's drunk. And high altitude will get you drunk faster than anything.

So, Ty and I finished up that first trip with a set of real happy campers. In fact, several weeks later, Bob sent me a copy of a letter from our people. They were very pleased and apparently thought both Ty and I could walk on water. This led to two more trips for Reds that summer and finally to being sent on a big trip where I was supposed to train all his other cooks, guaranteed to make you the least favorite employee in the outfit.

So, over the next ten years I contracted trips with Reds and most of the other outfits on the East Side of the sierras, including Reds, Agnew, North Lake, Cottonwood, Onion Valley, Frontier, and Rock Creek. Well, this is getting' a bit long so I better save the rest of the stories about Reds for another campfire. Good night and Happy Trails till then.

ART THE WONDER HORSE

Most horsemen consider the term "dude horse" to be an insult. If you take a polished show horse, highly sensitive to leg and rein cues, and you put him to work going down the sierra trails for 4 or 5 years, you will discover that he has become hard mouthed and resistant to most leg and rein signals. Your first reaction would be that he has been ruined. And you would be wrong. He has simply learned a new set of skills which allow him to survive and often to save his inexperienced rider from disaster.

Once, at Mt Whitney Pack Trains, I was leading a day ride up the first couple of miles of the Whitney trail. One of my guests was a 12-year-old boy who was riding Dooley, a big bay standardbred. Starting for home after our turn-around we were headed down a fairly steep hill in the tall pines. There was a switchback every 40 feet or so. Dooley's rider was obviously having trouble on the turns. As I watched I was horrified to see that instead of letting Dooley make the turns on his own or helping him by pulling the rein to the inside, his rider was taking the outside rein and pulling it as hard as he could to the outside. Dooley set his jaw against the bit and walked safely around the switchback. I stopped and explained to the kid that he should pull to the inside. On the next turn, he repeated his attempt to pull his horse off the mountainside. Again, Dooley saved both their lives by ignoring the reins. This time I yelled at the kid to put the reins down and let the horse alone. The next switchback was a repeat of the first two. This time I got off, took

Dooley's bridle off, and hitched a lead rope to his halter. Then I led our guest the rest of the way to the station. Dooley gave me this big sigh of relief that horses do when the danger is over. At the station the kid was almost in tears. He told me how a friend's dad had taught him how to neck rein by pulling the rein in the direction opposite the way he wanted to go. Thank heavens Dooley was one of those old, hard jawed, dude horses that ignored the bridle.

Years later when working for Red's Meadow I learned to really appreciate some of those dude horses. First you need to understand that part of the job of anybody working for a pack train is to ride the problem horses. That meant you rode anything that wasn't safe for guests such as new horses, young green-broke stock, old sour stock, buckers, runaways, or some that were too slow to keep up. Working for Bob Tanner at Reds, the most dreaded words I could hear were Bob saying, "Irene! Have I got a good horse for you!" One he gave me was so bad that when it ran away and left me afoot half way through a five-day trip, I was glad.

I eventually learned to cope with Bob's tendency to bless me with one more outlaw by beating him out to the corrals. When I would show up at the station, the first thing I would do was head for the corrals and pick out a good dude horse and saddle it up. When Bob would come to show me the new "good horse" he had for me, I would look all innocent and say, "Shucks Bob, I already saddled that other one. And my saddle's too heavy for a crippled-up old lady like me to resaddle." Usually he would let me get away with it.

When I had my choice, my favorite horse at Reds was Art, a 17-hand, gray, draft cross gelding. He was such a great horse that I usually referred to him as Art the Wonder Horse. Since I was short and fat, I would have to stand him next to a really large log or rock in order to get on him. Part of his appeal was that you could park him by a huge log and he would just patiently stand there waiting while you scrambled up the log to get on.

One time I was riding good ol' Art and leading a group of guests along the John Muir Trail next to upper Rush Creek. We stopped for a break and while some riders went in the bushes, the rest stayed on their mounts or got off to stretch their legs. I was just sitting there on Art, keeping an eye on everything. He was so huge that I usually didn't get off if I didn't have to. One rider was off with his horse's reins hooked over his saddle horn. That horse was trying to get his head down for a bite of grass. Being unable to do so pissed him off so he started pawing the ground. As luck would have it, he stuck one leg through the fastened reins. Jerking on his own mouth with his trapped leg, he panicked and started lunging around among the other people and animals. His rider jumped in the middle of things trying to save the horse. The horse started striking at him with his forefeet. It all happened in seconds.

Still sitting on Art, my only lucid thought was that it was my job to fix this. The next thing I knew, I was standing next to the problem horse. His foot was free, his bridle rein was cut in half, and I had my belt knife open in my hand. I was talkin' quiet to him and he was settling right down. While I checked the horse and rider over for damage, I looked to see what had become of Art. He was standing waiting exactly where I left him. I still don't remember what I had done, probably took a flying leap, crashed through people and horses while drawing my knife, and slashed the rein as soon as I could reach it. But the one thing I do know is that Art never moved one single inch through it all. Of course, later I got lambasted by the boss for cutting the rein. Oh, well.

Art's most amazing moment came one day when Ty Atwater and I were packing a trip out from above Shadow Lake. Art and I were riding in the lead and it was one of those miserable days with cold rain and howling wind. Back in those days all I could afford for rain gear was the infamous $2.99 plastic poncho from the sporting goods store, you know, the same ones that usually were flapping all over the hiker's backpacks.

Just so you can get an idea of how this all went, I'll give you a little description of where we were. Shadow Lake is along the Muir Trail above the steep walls of the canyon that encloses the headwaters of the San Joaquin River. We were on the trail that leaves the Muir, drops down into the canyon then climbs back up to Agnew Pack Station on the other side. The trail is cut into the cliff along the left side of the outlet and ends in a blind turn onto the canyon wall. The creek has dropped away under you to a small pool 50 feet straight down from the turn. Immediately past that pool is a 100-foot waterfall. The turn has maybe an extra eight inches on the outside edge of the trail between you and a fall that is guaranteed fatal.

So, Art the Wonder Horse is about 6 feet from the blind turn when two backpackers appear out of nowhere. In one split second the hikers take a single panicked look at the giant horse in front of them and jump onto the eight-inch ledge above the waterfall. At the same time, I jerk Art to a stop knowing that if we try to go on, it will mean the death of the hikers teetering on the ledge.

Of course, right now you are thinking, "Big deal. She'll just keep her horse quiet while she talks the hikers off the point and back down the trail to safety." Sounds easy, but how about if you couldn't see? Or how about if your horse couldn't see? Or how about if neither of you could see? How about if at that exact moment a violent gust of wind lifted your poncho over your head and jerked it down over your face and over your horse's head? Those of you who are experienced horsemen know that those ponchos scare the hell out of most horses when they just see them at a distance let alone when they have one thrown over their head.

I had told Art to stop and he did. He didn't spook at the sudden appearance of the hikers. He never moved when they jumped off the trail. He never even flinched when the poncho leaped into the air and came crashing down on his head, blinding him. I hunched forward over his neck and grabbed the part of the poncho that was on his head. He stayed dead still as I worked it off of his eyes and ears. Holding my breath, I slowly sat back up and pulled the poncho back over my head. Then I stood in the stirrups and pulled the tail of the poncho under my big, fat butt and sat on the damn thing. Now, let's see it blow away!

Checking out the rest of the situation, I saw that hikers were standing unmoving on the tiny ledge, and Art was still frozen exactly where I had stopped him. At this point I told the hikers that they should get back on the trail, walk back down around the corner and keep going until they reached a place where they could safely get off the trail and let us by. I looked back at my packer, Ty, and he gave me that sickly grin and nervous laugh that meant, "Oh, my gawd! I thought you guys were all going to die." Then I nudged Art with my heels and we went on down the trail like nothing had ever happened. And I thought, "definitely Art the Wonder Horse!"

Many years later I was having a bragging contest with Mary Jefferson, another backcountry cook who was related to practically everyone in these stories. I started telling stories about Art and then she was telling about a big, gray, draft cross gelding she had used when she worked for Art Schober at North Lake Pack Station. His name was Puppy Paws and she insisted he was the better horse. She had some fine stories about the great things he did on the trail. So, of course, I had to keep coming up with tales about Art. This went on until Mary allowed as how North Lake had to sell Puppy Paws because he was just too big for most of the dudes. When I asked her where he went, she went in the other room to ask Tommy. She came back and said he had gone to Reds Meadow. The truth hit both of us at the same time. Art and Puppy Paws were the same horse. When Tanner bought him, the wranglers had renamed him after the guy Bob bought him from, a common practice. And of course, his former owner at North Lake was Art Schober. So, Puppy Paws became Art and continued his career as one of the great dude horses of all time.

BOOKS?

High in the land of beauty and adventure, it seems unlikely that a pack train employee would crave quiet time alone with a book. However, I myself am a voracious reader and I know that many other denizens of the high sierra are also. I try to never leave for the mountains without 5 or 6 books. I read mostly quick, easy reads like westerns, romances, or science fiction. When I run out, I often trade or borrow books with my fellow packer-folk or with the guests. Some of the best books I have ever read were loaned to me by my guests. On the opposite end of things, there have been times when I was desperate enough for reading material to read the label on the oatmeal box.

In my entire life I have pretty much finished every book I started. Once when I was in the hospital after surgery, I tried to read "Shogun" but it was too long and I was too sick. The only other book I didn't finish was Michener's "Poland." I really enjoyed it at first. Wonderful writing and pastoral characters that you quickly became attached to. Apparently, Poland's entire history consists of repeated invasions which resulted in wiping out the whole population. The country has no natural geographic defenses so as soon as the new population got settled, someone else would come along and wipe them out. It was so depressing that when it reached the 1880's, I promised myself that the 30 years between that time and the start of World War I had better be peaceful or I would throw the damn book away. I turned the next page, and they were being invaded again. I sat by the campfire and fed the pages to the flames. So much for that book.

Actually, no matter how tired I am I can't go to sleep at night without having something to read first even if it's only a few pages. Once when I spent a week with a group of FFA high school students at the Junior Livestock Fair in Bishop, I forgot to bring anything to read. The first night I tossed and turned the whole night. The next night at bedtime, I counted kids and discovered one of my best students, Tressa, was missing. I waited up a good half hour and she finally returned. Getting ready to chew her out for sneaking off, I finally realized that she was carrying a large armful of magazines. She handed them to me and said, "Here. I went out and borrowed these from all the other students and coaches here. None of us can stand to listen to you thrashing around for another night."

Many years ago, back in the 60's when I was working for Mount Whitney, we were on a big, long trip in the southern sierra. Norrie Livermore was our head packer and he had a paperback copy of "Catch 22." It had just come out, but it wouldn't have been a big deal except that Norrie was reading it while he was on the trail with his string. He was riding in the lead and every few minutes he would start laughing and keep right on laughing until he was doubled over in the saddle. At the end of the day we would all beg him to tell us what was so funny. He would share some of the better moments from the book and soon we were all hooked. Eventually he got tired of having to constantly retell the book. So, since he was several chapters along, he tore out the first chapter and gave it to one of the other packers. That packer read the first chapter, passed it on to another packer, and got the next chapter from Norrie. After a while everyone was reading a different chapter and passing it on down the line. We must have been a sight, leading strings or dudes down the trail, each of us with a piece of the book in our hands, laughing like a bunch of demented hyenas. Then came the day of the great book disaster. After a long, hard move we arrived in camp where Norrie made the discovery that he had lost the book. During the hard part of the move, when it wasn't possible to read, he had stuffed the book in his back pocket. It must have fallen out as it was now gone. Deep depression settled over the crew as we pondered our situation. Many people made suggestions for retrieving the book, but none of them were actually possible. It would be fun to make this incident longer and more complicated, but truth-be-told right then a backpacker came down the trail. He walked into our camp, pulled something out of his pocket and said, "Did anybody here lose a book? I found it on the trail. Since you guys were ahead of me, I thought it might belong to one of you. It's pretty tore up, but if any of you want it you sure can have it." Norrie quickly retrieved the book and the entire crew offered the backpacker anything we had to show our gratitude. Since he apparently had no use for anyone's lifeblood or first born child, he just accepted an invitation to join us for dinner.

Another funny book story happened years later up on Mono Creek. I was working for Rock Creek Pack and we were doing a ten-day packing school at the beginning of the summer. This trip was crewed by the boss, Craig London, one experienced packer, and one old cook. All the new crew (both packers and cooks) was there to be trained for the summer and there were a few guests that were there because they wanted a chance to learn that packin' stuff. This trip was designed with a lot of short moves and layover days to allow a lot of time for training and practicing. That meant I could look forward to quite a bit of reading time. Unfortunately, when I packed up at home, I realized that I was out of books. With the exception of my husband's books, I didn't have one single book that I hadn't already read. How can I explain my husband's books? Being the hardest working guy, I ever knew, he doesn't have a whole lot of time to read. But when he does read, he reads what I call "dirty westerns." They are short, trashy little books written to a formula. They are all about 200 pages long, include quite a bit of violence, and include three fairly explicit sex scenes; one in the first chapter, one in the middle of the book, and one about two chapters before the bloody shootout at the end of the book. Like I said, I'll read anything, so I grabbed up a handful of those and threw them in my dunnage.

So, several days later laid over at Widowmaker Camp on Mono Creek, I had just finished one of those books when it was time to start dinner. My bedroll was laid out just next to my kitchen, so I dropped the book on top of the bed as I started to work on dinner. Before too long one of the guests came by. I don't actually know his name, but his friends called him "Gunther the Bavarian" and he had a heavy German accent. This is only important because you may not know that for the last 150 years many, many Germans have been completely nuts over cowboys and Indians. In fact, some of the world's finest collections of Native American artifacts are in German museums. So. Gunther had spotted the book on my bedroll. Hovering over it he began to ask questions. "Oh, it is a vestern." Yeah, he actually pronounced it vestern. "Is it yours? Have you finished it? May I borrow it?" The whole time I was trying to figure out how to tell him that this western was not exactly the same as the westerns he was used to. I carefully explained the sex and violence to him, but he still insisted on borrowing it.

I spent the next day worrying about Gunther and the dirty western. What if he was offended, or upset enough to complain to the boss? Gunther was a real nice guy that all the guests and crew really liked. Not the kind of person you wanted to upset. Sure enough, next afternoon, Gunther marched angrily into my kitchen with the book in his hand. My first thought was that I had accidentally offended a guest. I don't mind offending people, but only when I mean to. Gunther threw the book on the bedroll and as my heart sank, he turned to me and hissed, "This is not a vestern! This is PORNOGRAPHY!" Before I could explain or apologize, he stepped closer and looking around to see that we were alone he said, "Got any more?" I was laughing pretty hard while I dug through my dunnage to get him a couple more "dirty westerns." Seems like by the end of the trip he had borrowed and read most all of them.

LOVE IN THE HIGH LONESOME

The Sierra Nevada, if there was ever a place to fall in love, this is it. The sky is so clear and blue that if you painted a picture of it as it actually is, no one would believe it. At night that same sky is a black velvet blanket ablaze with millions of stars, layer upon layer of them twinkling off into infinity. Under a full moon the canyon walls are a black and white photo of pines standing stark in their own shadows against the white slabs of moon-washed granite.

Yep, pretty much everyone in the high lonesome is in love. But truth be told, what they are actually in love with is the mountains themselves. Eventually everyone there makes the mistake of thinking these feelings are really for another person. For a short time, the lucky packer-person-in-love floats around surrounded by beauty and joy on all sides. It's a little tough for their fellow workers as someone is bound to have to pick up the work they miss in the process. A few are lucky enough to find a lifelong relationship with someone who loves the high lonesome as they do. The majority go through a period of infatuation before they realize that the object of their affections is somewhat less perfect than they had imagined. Unfortunately, by this time the boss, trying to be nice, has partnered the two "lovers" together on the job. After that, the breaking up period becomes ugly for all concerned.

One of the more memorable break-ups at Rock Creek Pack was between Kelly and Jim. They were both great people, just not when they were together. They were married so the break-up took several summers resulting eventually in the infamous mule-shit/chewing-tobacco incident. Like I said these conflicts can be pretty hard on the rest of the crew who can eventually become sick and tired of the whole thing. At the time in question Rock Creek had three camps located along Davis Lake in the Hilton Lakes Basin. My camp was in the middle. Kelly's was about 100 yards to the left. And the camp where Jim was packing was about ¼ mile away to the right just past the outlet. The guests in the camps knew each other and were having a joint party at my camp on the night in question. Kelly was still working at her camp, but Jim was in my camp drinking and dancing with the guests. Jim was in hot pursuit of a young, blonde, lady lawyer. As the evening wore on their kissing and groping became pretty blatant, and all the rest of the crew was hoping that Kelly wouldn't come over to our camp. Boy howdy, would that have been ugly. Eventually Jim came over to the rest of the crew to borrow some chew. He was one of those guys who quit chewing 10 years ago and had borrowed from everyone ever since. After he got some from Bottiani and walked away, the rest of the crew was expressing some pretty negative feelings.

We decided that there wasn't anything we could do about his romance, but there might be something we could do to stump break him from scrounging chew. Mike donated the rest of his pouch of chew. Fred went to the picket line for some fresh mule manure. I took out about ½ of the chew and put it in a ziplock for Mike. The boys mixed the rest of the chew with an equal amount of manure and put it back in the pouch. About 30 minutes later, Jim returned to borrow more chew. Mike gave him the whole pouch and told him to just keep it. We all watched in horror as Jim took some of the tobacco/manure mixture and chewed it. Then he took some more and so on until it was all gone. Jim was so drunk that he didn't realize what was going on until several days later when one of the boys started making fun of him for chewing mule shit. But the really startling thing was that the blonde lawyer lady was also so drunk that she kept right on making out with Jim while they were dancing. That eventually resulted in the Rock Creek quintessential unanswered question, "How drunk do you have to be to kiss a guy who is chewing mule shit?" Still no answer to that, but it's a great question.

The next day around camp, I kept hearing strange comments from both crew and guests. One guy was returning to the Outlet Camp very late and found a very drunk Jim staggering along the trail headed away from his own camp. Figuring Jim was lost in the dark, that kind soul guided him back to his camp. Even later another guest found Jim again headed away from Outlet Camp. When he tried to help, Jim told him to let him be. So that guy left Jim staggering south toward the camp that contained both Kelly and the little blonde lawyer. Don't know for sure how that turned out, but the next morning a crew member from that camp told me that he had found a camp chair by the fire ring that was crushed all flat as if more than one person had been in it at a time. Always kinda figured that Jim musta found whatever he was lookin' for.

Soon after the chew incident Jim and Kelly went their separate ways and seemed to both find much better lives apart than they had had together. The period when a romance is winding down through the bickering and fighting stage is terrible for the couple, but even worse for the rest of the crew who has to work with them. Let's just say that you can't really depend on people whose personal lives are in turmoil, but I'll save that story for another evening.

Romance takes many forms in the high lonesome. The most embarrassing I remember was the time my guests and I rode up on a trail repair site near Grassy Lake. There was a young guy ranger assigned to Grassy Lake being helped by a young female ranger who had hiked over Goodale Pass from Graveyard Meadow to help with the trail work. I was leading a group of riders heading down from Grassy to Jackson Meadow on the way to Cascade Valley and was the first to discover that the two rangers working on the repair had taken a little "romance" break right in the middle of the trail. They had removed a giant boulder from the trail, and I could see two naked bodies entwined in the bottom of the hole where the rock used to be. Noticing two green USFS uniforms discarded by the side of the trail I jerked my mule into an abrupt turn into the trees and led my guests down to another less embarrassing section of trail. As far as I could tell most of my guests failed to notice the inappropriate activities in the trail. Later one guest asked why I had cut across that section and I truthfully said that there was a big hole in the trail.

Truth be told there were times when your old cook and storyteller fell into this same romance traps all the way from incredible to ridiculous, but if you think I'm gonna tell you about them here, you are sadly mistaken. Most everybody ends up looking ridiculous in these situations and I look that way plenty often enough without putting myself in that position here.

Even funnier than some of these stories was one beautiful evening out by the horse corrals at Whitney Portals when I found a young Mt Whitney packer, also named Jim, gazing into a pair of lovely brown eyes as he softly recited love poetry to a big bay mare named Dorothy. With that picture in mind, it seems like a good time to leave the campfire for another evening and snuggle down in our sleeping bags to sweet sierra dreams.

ADVENTURES WITH ONE GIANT MULE

In the old days in the mountains, women were usually cooks, kitchen help, day ride girls or wranglers. On the trail you usually got to babysit the guest riders. Being pretty vain, I always preferred to get to lead some mules. That way everyone would know that you were a hand and no one would mistake you for a dude. The best deal was if you got to lead a whole string of five mules. That got you some respect, especially if you did it well.

At Rock Creek Pack Trains, it was a Henkes hiking trip where I got to lead a full string of 5 for 15 days. Craig London decided that the crew we had was so good that the three of us could do a job that would normally require a crew of five. Craig had been packing a full string since he was seven, was a veterinarian, and was pretty damn good at anything he set his mind to. The other packer was Matt Raven, outstanding horseman, long time packer, polo player, and world class educator in the equine world. I was the third member of the crew and was one of the best backcountry cooks, pretty good with a string of mules, and ancient enough to talk with our rather elderly guests. My job was to cook for 20 and lead one of the strings. The boys teamed up to pack my mules as there was no way in hell that I could lift 90-pound side loads, especially on to 16 and 17 hand mules. Meanwhile I cooked, tore down camp, and got the loads together. One of the funniest parts of this trip was that the boys would dress in T shirts, jeans and tennis shoes to saddle and pack the 15 head of mules, and saddle the three riding animals. When the packing was all done, Craig would yell go and he and Matt would race in taking off their working clothes and putting on their boots, spurs, chaps, western shirts, belts and buckles, wild rags and cowboy hats. It was laughingly referred to as the "cowboy accessory race."

It was on this trip that I first met Art, a mule that at 17 hands was truly one giant mule. He was a light draft cross who had already been with the outfit a long time when I first met him. He was a tall, raw-boned, light bay. He was pretty dependable on the trail, but I didn't start out with any great affection for him. He was pretty similar to two of the best mules in the outfit, Henry and Alice. I always kinda assumed that they had all come to Rock Creek as part of the same string or at least from the same source. Since the other two were so outstanding, they were discussed a lot by the crew. Nobody had all that much to say about Art. My first memorable meeting with Art was on the bluffs along the Muir Trail above Palisades Lakes. Being on the edge of the meadow, my mules were taking the opportunity to grab a few bites of grass. As often happened, this led to them stepping over each other's lead ropes and getting all tangled up. By the time I knew we were in trouble, the next mule's lead rope went from Art's shoulder, under his belly, twice around his off hind leg, and then under the next mule's left foreleg. They were all standing right on the edge of the bluff where it dropped off to the lake. So, there was no way to get to the mules from their off side. Figuring that I didn't have time to untie the rope, and knowing that cutting the rope was frowned on by the management, I came to the not-so-brilliant idea that I might be able to crawl under the giant mule and unwrap the rope by hand. I crawled under Art's belly, picked up his hind leg, unwrapped the rope, laid it on the ground between his back legs, crawled back to the next mule, picked up that mule's left fore, got the rope over on his left side, ducked under his head, went forward to Art, lifted his left hind and pulled the rope back into place. I was so thrilled with my success that I felt like yelling Yahoo. Then I caught the look on Art's face. He was quietly standing there with his head turned around watching me. His face plainly said, "Are you through fooling around under there? I been waiting patiently here for you, but I think we should go now." Trying not to look sheepish, I quickly got back on my horse and we rode off down the trail, one packer and her string of mules.

Several years later I spent some time on another trip with Art. It was a long trip in the Southern Sierra with a group of riders, most of whom had packed with us before. I wasn't leading a string that time. Our head packer was Dave Dohnel, one of the partners in the outfit. Second packer was a friend of Dave's named Mike Dufresne. And of course, cooking and wrangling was the old lady, Irene. This was my first big trip with my personal mule, Julie. She had come to me through the Mule Days sale off of a truck load of mules from Texas. She was a round, stocking legged, red mule who eventually became the absolute best of mules. But at this point she was pretty much of a brat who took lots of spurring to make her go and then bucked when she was spurred. On the day we moved from the pines and deep grass of Little Whitney Meadow 2,000 feet down the canyon wall to the Kern River, I wasn't paying a lot attention to Art or any of the other pack animals, especially when I lost a Chicago screw out of Julie's bridle and it fell right off her head. I had to lead her most of the way down the steep trail into the canyon. Just before we got to the bottom, I found a piece of pink electrical wire, probably left there from a trail crew using explosives in trail repair. Though it looked pretty silly, it made a fine bridle repair and I got to get my tired feet out of the dust and into the stirrups.

Being around 7,000 foot elevation on the floor of the canyon, we pushed through a lot of dry brush and listened to the rattlesnakes singing all around us. Soon we came to the bridge over the Kern River near Lewis Camp. It had been a wet year and the river was higher than I had ever seen it. It was deep enough to drown a horse as it roared and crashed through car-sized boulders. It was for periods of run-off like this that the bridge had been built. It was a suspension bridge that was barely one pack mule wide. On suspension bridges you have to separate the mules from the strings because if they walk in unison the vibrations tear up the bridge. This bridge had a bizarre railing designed so the pack loads would ride up on it and slide all the way across the bridge on it.

When it came to Art's turn to cross the bridge, no one expected trouble as he had quietly crossed dozens of them in his life and never been a problem. Mike lead him and he walked right on until he got to the start of the railing where he suddenly stopped, acted like he was struggling to go forward, then panicked and ran backwards off the bridge. Dave and I came to help herd him onto the bridge for another try.

The results were the same, only by now Art was shaking, sweating, and rolling his eyes in fear. On the third try we finally realized that what was happening was that his huge duffle loads hung so low that they couldn't ride up onto the railing. We were asking the poor guy to do something that couldn't be done and he was terrified. Dave unpacked him so we could lead him across. Unfortunately, poor old Art wasn't having any part of that. He had been so frightened by the whole thing that he had decided he wasn't setting foot on that bridge come hell or high water.

After several failed tries, Dave decided that the only way to get him across the river was to swim him across. Dave's riding horse was a three-year-old, green broke mustang. So he traded Dufresne for Rusty, a strong, sensible older gelding. As they led Art into the roaring, foaming water, I realized that Dave might not have a clear exit from the other side of the river. I ran across the bridge and along the bank until I found a way out for them. I waved to Dave and watched in awe as he and Rusty pulled Art across that raging torrent. To picture this, try to imagine the wildest video of white water rafting you have ever seen. Nothing was above the water but the heads of the animals and Dave's torso. The water was throwing them around among huge boulders that reached much higher out of the water than they did. Finally they reached the bank and struggled out of the water. It was about the bravest thing I'd ever seen or possibly the craziest. As he and the animals stood dripping on the river bank, Dave talked like it was no big deal. Then he led Art back to this side of the bridge while Mike dragged the loads across. While they were repacking Art, the guests came back from the places they had been watching from during the great swim. One of them said he had filmed it. Dave shrugged his shoulders and said it was just part of the job. With the animals reloaded, we rode on to that night's camp. About a year later, Dave told me that he had seen the guy's film and it made him realize that the river was a whole lot worse than he had imagined. He sounded like he might be reconsidering the "no big deal" outlook.

The next day we continued up canyon. We had made a few changes in the stock. Dave was riding my little mule so he could give her a few lessons involving spurs and bucking. I was riding Dave's mustang, Shelby. He was a 16-hand red gelding out of the Susanville herd. He only had about eight months riding in him. Dave usually started a couple of mustangs each winter while waiting for it to be summer in the sierras again. Shelby was quite a horse and Dave was a better trainer than I had imagined. When you are riding a green colt in the high country and discover you can steer him with you little finger, you have to be impressed.

All went well until we reached the crossing on Rattlesnake Creek. This was another bridge, but a much easier one. It was fairly new, built of flattened logs, and wide enough to drive a car across. It was the kind of bridge that no one ever had trouble with, so we were all caught by surprise when Art decided that this might not be the same bridge but by gosh it was a bridge and he WASN'T doing it. He was big enough that when he pulled back, he almost wrecked the whole outfit. We had loose mules and lost loads everywhere. In a case like that I often end up as the horse holder. While the guys were catching up and fixing loads, I served as a spare hitching rack. Eventually I ended up standing there holding Art. I explained to him that he was a bad mule and nobody much liked him right now. We stood there a long time and the more I talked to him the more he relaxed. That would have been a good deal except that we still had to get him across the bridge. As I talked and talked, the glaze of fear gradually left his eyes. I explained to him that if he would just walk quietly over the bridge everything would be okay. At that point he let out a big sigh and rested his chin on my shoulder. I sighed too and muttering, "Oh, what the hell," started walking slowly toward the bridge. He followed along like we were out for a stroll in the meadow. With me stroking his nose and talking foolishness, we crossed the bridge like it wasn't even there. Even better, the next day when he was back with his string, he crossed a big bridge on the main river just like he had never had a problem. Guess he remembered that he really was a good mule.

Years later when Art was likely pushing 30, we were on a similar trip in the southern sierra. Our guests were German hikers and "peak baggers" who were there to 'summit' the four listed peaks on the Kern Plateau. It had been a real wet winter and the Forest Service had closed all the meadows in that area to stock grazing. That meant that we had to feed our animals hay cubes that were hauled to us daily by pack strings from Cottonwood Pack Station. We also had to hand water them. As someone who has now reached a somewhat advanced age, I can appreciate that Art's digestive system could no longer deal with dry feed and a limited amount of water. As might be expected, by the fourth day of the trip Art was showing symptoms of colic. We tried several traditional remedies, but nothing seemed to help. When he went three straight days without producing any manure, we guessed that he had an intestinal blockage. Bad, bad news. He also quit being able to pee. Needless to say, he was completely miserable. When we camped at Templeton Meadow, the only thing we hadn't tried was a shot of banamine. No such luck. When you are trying to put an IV shot in a 1300-pound, 17 hand mule and he doesn't want you to, there is no question who will win. Lying awake all night I tried desperately to think my way out of this. I knew that it wouldn't be much longer before the only way out would be to put him down. Our head packer Jason carried a loaded pistol for just such emergencies, but I hated to even think about it.

Finally, in the wee small hours of the morning, I came up with an idea. In most cases of blockage there is nothing you can do since mules and horses have about a hundred feet of intestines and there is no way to reach 95% of it. BUT, what if the blockage was in the last three feet of gut? And wasn't that where the blockage would have to be if it was pressing on the urethra enough to cut off the urine flow? I had raised horses most of my life which meant I had done rectal palpations on pregnant mares. What the heck, it was worth a try.

Before first light I explained the plan to the packers. Probably humoring the old cook they agreed to help me give it a try. I scrubbed up and used the dish soap for a lubricant. Using all their strength, the boys backed Art up to a big log so I could stand on something tall enough to reach under the big mule's tail. Poor old guy was so miserable that he didn't even react to what I was doing to him. Only about 18 inches in I came to the blockage and started scooping it out. Altogether it was about the size of a big loaf of bread and took quite a while to clear out. When I couldn't reach any more, the boys led Art away while I climbed off the log. None of us knew if we had actually done him any good or not. He took a few more steps, stopped and started to pee. It looked like he peed out about 5 gallons. The look on his face was pure relief. That answered the question of whether we had cleared the urethra. The boys took Art down to the stream for a drink then turned him out in the meadow. He gave a big sigh and started munching on the wet meadow grass. Trying not to cry like a fool, I quickly started washing up my hands and arms.

Figured I better get them clean before the guests came for coffee and saw what my hands had been doing before I cooked their breakfast.

So that's the end of Art's adventures. He was fine for the rest of the trip and our boss, Dr. London, made sure he didn't take any more trips that required dry feed. Our guests happily bagged all four peaks they were after. Going down to the Kern River I was amazed to discover that Jason was afraid of rattlesnakes. When our guests found out about our problem with Art, they wanted to know what we would have done if we hadn't been able to save him. When I explained that we would have put him down, they wanted to know how. So Jason went and got his pistol to show them. They were absolutely horrified. Apparently, no one, and I mean NO ONE, in Germany owns a gun. When they realized that all three of us either had a gun with us or had some at home, they reacted as if they were surrounded by wolves. The whole rest of the trip they kept glancing at us as if we might attack them at any moment.

The funniest post script to this story came later when I told Craig about Art's tribulations. I must admit I was pretty puffed up and bragging a bit. Being as Craig is both the boss of Rock Creek and a genuine veterinarian, I expected him to be grateful and maybe even impressed by how we saved his mule. When I got to the part about getting up on the log and sticking my arm up Art's butt, Craig gasped and said, "Oh, no. I wouldn't ever have done that." Being as he was a vet and I was an amateur, I figured I might have endangered the animal by my ignorance. I asked Craig what he meant, and this 6'8" professional vet said, "Art hates to have anyone mess with his back end. I'da been scared to do that!" I guess I was just too dumb to know that wasn't a good idea.

FIRST MUSTANG TRIP IN THE PIZONA

Mustang trips start at River Springs on Adobe Flats. You haul the guests out from Bishop to a barren alkali flat between Mono Lake and the Nevada border. You drive across 60 some miles of lonesome country as the road grows narrower, rougher, and dustier. You pass hay ranches, cattle outfits, hot springs and ghost towns. You finally reach the remains of an 1870's stage station at River Springs. The springs are still there and gushing fresh water out onto the dry flats at the base of a set of low, rolling volcanic hills. The remains of the station include the barely upright bunkhouse, broken-down corrals, and a large round corral built of dry-stack walls of black lava. Surprisingly, the round corral is still usable. We often hold our riding animals there between trips.

It's real wild country. The Pizona is sage flats and pinyon covered hills rising eastward to the Nevada border, Montgomery Pass, and finally to Boundary Peak, the highest mountain in Nevada. Only about 30 miles due west looms the massive granite wall of the Sierra Nevada Mountains. In mid- May the sierras are still blanketed in last winter's snow with all the trails completely impassable to stock. That is why Rock Creek Pack Trains, its horses, mules and crew were here camping out and leading guests to observe mustang bands in the wild.

The first season I actually worked the Pizona full time, we started out with a fairly thin crew. Craig London, our boss, and Tom Alawelt, a longtime packer, were the only two who actually knew their way around that country, the wild horses, and the other wildlife there. The rest of the crew was a cook who thought he was last of the great outdoor cooks, and two cowboys from West Texas who knew a lot about stock but very little about this kind of country. For the first time, I got to be mule-back hunting mustangs and didn't have to be in the kitchen hardly at all. Boy was I looking forward to that.

As the first trip of the season we started out from Benton Hot Springs with a couple of short warm-up days followed by a long cross country move to the Pizona camp. Then we had a single day looking for mustangs from Upper Pizona to McBride followed by a final move out to River Springs where all the rest of our trips would start

Things didn't get real challenging until we headed up to McBride. We had about 15 guests with Tom in the lead studying the tracks and teaching the guests the hand signals that would allow us to communicate without the mustangs hearing us. Chris and Jed, the boys from Texas, were riding a couple of green colts, watching the dudes, and trying to learn the country. I was riding drag and leading a single pack mule which carried about 8 gallons of water, everyone's lunches and any equipment that our folks didn't have room for on their horses. The boss wasn't with us as he had to go back to Bishop to haul additional supplies into the Pizona camp. Craig had told me to watch the boys and pass the mule on to whichever of them seemed comfortable on his new animal first. About five miles out, near McNamara Lake, I passed the mule on to Chris as he and Quantum seemed to getting along pretty good. Jed's colt, Cactus, was a little younger and there was a kinda shadow in Jed's eyes that said he might need a little more time before he was ready to lead a mule off of the colt.

We climbed the next ridge toward McBride but Tom still wasn't getting any fresh mustang tracks. We'd seen some fresh bear tracks and a two-day old lion kill, but no horses. At this point Tom explained we would continue up to McBride and then to the pass to stop for lunch. Since that meant we would miss Horse Flat on the other side of the ridge, Tom decided to send someone to check there for sign. He sent Jed as Chris was leading the mule. He told Jed, "Ride over the ridge to the flat, make a circle, then meet us on the pass." We watched Jed disappear over the ridge with Cactus objecting every step of the way. We had no idea that it might be awhile before we saw either of them again.

Eventually we stopped for lunch in a grove of pinyon trees on McBride Pass. During lunch we entertained our guests with a look at some nearby petroglyphs and a spot on the ridge just covered in chips of obsidian left from working arrowheads. No doubt this had once been a Paiute campsite.

We waited a long time but Jed never rejoined us. Figuring that he might have gotten in trouble with the colt, we headed back toward camp by way of Horse Flat. We figured we would find Jed, Cactus, or hopefully both of them. At worst we should find their tracks. Tom was, of course, leading as neither Chris nor I had ever been there before. In the southeast corner of Horse Flat, Tom Found Jed's tracks. He was walking and leading his horse. His tracks were pretty distinctive as he was a short guy with small feet. Pretty much a case of following tracks of itty, bitty cowboy boots. Unfortunately, those tracks were leading away from anywhere he might have wanted to be. Once you get lost in the Pizona, you are in real trouble. It all looks alike; sagebrush covered flats, pinyon covered hills, more flats, more hills, and they all look the same.

So, Tom needed to find Jed, but Tom was the only one who could guide our group back to camp. Looked like it could be a problem. Tom, Chris and I got off away from the dudes and discussed our situation. Chris was now riding drag and responsible for the mule and its load. I was now the leader and would pretend I knew where we were going. Tom said things like, "Rim around the west end of this flat until you find an old road heading southwest. Follow the road until you can see the lake. Then take the left fork and go over two ridges. Just before the road bends right, find a basalt ridge. Show the guests the petroglyphs on the basalt and give them a pee break. I will catch up to you there and tell you where to go next." Unbelievably, this way he managed to search for Jed and get us back to camp safely, popping up repeatedly just when I needed him. Unfortunately, he ran out of daylight before he could find Jed whose tracks continued to lead farther away from us with every step.

Back at camp, the guests were having dinner and worrying about Jed. Just as it was getting dark, Tom returned with the bad news that he hadn't found him. His tracks showed that he and Cactus weren't hurt, just lost and heading the wrong direction. The new cook whose experience with this kind of work was pretty limited, started pacing around camp loudly voicing his opinion that we should send a truck to the nearest phone and call out a search and rescue team from Pickle Meadows Marine Base. We told him that we couldn't do anything like that until the boss arrived from town which should be any minute. Not slowed down a bit, the cook announced that we should form our own search party. Since the number one rule of SARs is to never start a search in the dark, I tried to ignore him. I tried to point out that Jed and Cactus might be hungry and thirsty, but were most likely okay otherwise.

Finally, Craig arrived from town. After he and Tom assessed the situation, they came up with a pretty good plan. Chris and I were now in charge of the trip and the guests. The next day was the last day of their trip and we would take them to look for mustangs in the morning, then ride out to River Springs and use the company trucks to haul the people back to their vehicles at Benton Hot Springs. Tom would take his horse, the pack mule, and ten gallons of water to pick up Jed's tracks where he had run out of daylight before. Right now, Craig would drive back to Bishop where he would arrange for a pilot and plane to take him on a search pattern first thing in the morning.

The following day as Chris and I were finishing off this first trip, Craig and Tom were successful in finding Jed and returning him safely to camp. When we saw Jed there that evening, we got to hear the story of his great adventure. It, like so many disasters in life, was triggered by a simple failure to communicate. When Tom originally told Jed to take a circle to look for mustangs and then meet us on the ridge, what Tom meant was for Jed to circle around the edge of the flat which was about ½ mile away. He had no idea that the phrase "Take a circle" means something entirely different in West Texas than it does here. Where these Texas boys had been working cows "take a circle" meant ride out about ten miles, swing around in as big a loop as you could and still get back by dark. Trying to carry out what Jed understood as his directions must have been just about impossible. His horse, Cactus, was a green three-year-old who didn't want anything to do with this little sojourn in the wilderness. Tom said that their tracks showed that Jed was walking as often as he was riding.

So, Jed and Cactus had been thoroughly lost with no food, no water, and no idea which way was home. Finally, Cactus gave out and refused to move one more step. Jed was afraid if he turned him loose, he would be in trouble with the boss. Also, there was the chance that Cactus might try to join a wild band and the stud would kill him. So, Jed found a big shady pinyon pine, unsaddled Cactus and tied him there figuring that when he made it to safety, he could backtrack to pick up the horse.

Eventually Jed spotted what looked like it might be a camp in the distance, He had to scramble down some steep bluffs to get there but it was indeed a camp. The camp at Truman Meadows actually belonged to another pack outfit, and they must have been between trips as there was no one there. The camp didn't have much to offer, but when it's comin' on dark, a place that offers tents for shelter, a spring for water, and a dirt road headed toward civilization musta looked like heaven to poor Jed.

First thing the next morning Jed was outside a tent lookin' around and trying to decide what to do next when he heard a low flying plane scooting along over the hills. Hoping that it might be some kind of help, he ran out in the open jumping up and down and waving his hat. The plane circled back dipping his wings in a sign of recognition. Then it circled again and dropped a lunch sack full of food, some toilet paper, and a message telling Jed to wait there.

The plane returned to the Bishop Airport where Craig thanked Kirk Peek for the quickest search and rescue in history. Then Craig rented a short-wheel- based jeep and headed for the Pizona. The old dirt roads through that country are really rough, and he needed to pick up Jed, find Cactus and return over the top of the hills to our camp site in Lower Pizona. When Craig and Jed returned to camp, it was just getting dark and after spending all afternoon searching and backtracking, they had not found Cactus. A few minutes later Tom rode in from his search but his news wasn't any better. Poor old Cactus had now spent 2 days without feed or water. They planned to go out again the next day but it might well be Cactus's last chance.

At first light the next day Tom and Craig headed back out in search of one lost horse. As that morning was the beginning of our next trip, Jed, Chris, and I went to River Springs to pick up our new guests. We got everything saddled and our people a horseback. We rode into the hills and to the west where we showed them a small band of mustangs along the pole line road. Then we continued on several miles north to our camp. We spent the rest of the day taking care of the stock, getting the dudes settled in, and unloading the duffle and supplies from the

4-wheel drive truck that had hauled it the long way around to camp. The whole time all of us kept sneaking glances up canyon hoping to spot some sign of Tom or Craig.

After dinner but before dark, we finally spotted Tom riding down the creek leading his pack mule and one sorrel, three-year-old, draft-cross gelding. The whole crew took off for the creek crossing to greet the returning heroes. All things considered, Cactus looked pretty good. Tom explained that he had followed Jed's tracks all the way from Horse Flat to the other camp on Truman Meadows twice yesterday and again today with no luck. There was one place pretty far along where Jed had made a fair-sized circle to the left and then returning to his tracks, had continued on the direction he had been going. Something about this spot worried Tom so he returned to it yet again. He took a larger circle around it and found tracks heading off to the right. Hot damn, it wasn't a circle but a figure eight. Far out on the right loop was a big ol' pinyon with one thirsty, hungry, lonely red horse tied under it.

Fortunately, Tom knew what to do. The nearest water was about 5 miles away at Upper Pizona Springs. That, of course, is why Tom was leading a pack mule with ten gallons of water in his packs. Tom gave Cactus a couple of gallons of water then started back. Every few miles he would stop and unpack the mule to offer Cactus some more water. By the time they had covered the five miles to the springs, he managed to polish off the whole ten gallons. If he had given him all the water at once, he would have coliced and maybe even died. At the upper spring Tom let him drink as much as he wanted before they continued the four miles down canyon to our camp.

That night around the campfire there was some discussion of the meaning of "take a circle" and the difficulty of tracking a figure eight. Jed stayed pretty quiet as he was real embarrassed at having to be rescued. When Jed had been returned to camp the night before, you could see how Chris felt to find his best friend alive and well, but he didn't say anything, just shook his hand, slapped him on the shoulder, and went back to work. This night he and Jed didn't make any big deal about the last few days either 'cause that's the cowboy way.

NO DANGED HORSES

East of the High Sierra between Mono Lake and the Nevada Border lie Adobe Flats, Black Lake, River Springs, and the Pizona. This is the home of the Montgomery Pass wild horse herd. This herd is almost never together, but rather broken up in bands of one to twenty head of horses. In the spring when the trails in the high country are blocked with snow, Rock Creek takes groups of dudes on four- or five-day trips to watch the mustangs. When you're looking for mustangs in the Pizona, mostly what's important is to give your guests a chance to see the wild horses in the wild. These animals are ideal for that as they haven't been chased or gathered in the last fifty years. On most all the trips I took there we saw at least a few mustangs. On one trip we actually saw over one hundred head. If you drew a blank, you needed to be prepared to show them as much other interesting stuff as you could. This might include wild horse tracks and stud piles, bear and mountain lion tracks, some ancient Indian house rings and petroglyphs, the remains of a lion-killed foal, the ruins of a windmill from an early homestead, and the hundred-year-old ruins of the toll house on the old wagon road. But mostly you had to make them feel that they had been there and "seen the elephant."

Well, obviously, I'm working up to telling the story of the mustang trip where we didn't see any mustangs. On our first day we rode from River Springs to our camp at Lower Pizona. At River Springs we got our 24-some guests split into two groups, and matched with their horses. We adjusted saddles, lengthened stirrups, and gave basic riding directions.

I was guide for one group and another woman was guide for the second group. I'm not going to mention her name here, mostly just because I don't want to. She had just brought the previous day's group out from camp. There were two main routes from River Springs to camp, one leads northwest along the pole line road and the other climbs over the volcanic hills to the northeast. Since the other guide had just come in over the pole line road, I asked her if they had found any horses or sign out in that direction. She said that there wasn't anything out that way and that I should take the hill trail. She said that she would take the hill trail too. Since my group was supposed to leave half an hour ahead of hers, she asked us to be careful not to spook out any mustangs we saw.

Of course, we didn't see any horses. There weren't any horses, not even any tracks. Around the campfire that night we got to listen to the other guide brag about showing her guests a nice band of horses out on the pole line. Her people added to the story by telling all about the band of seven with the bay stud and the new red foal. They were real pleased with how smart their guide was as she took them straight to the horses. Seemed as how they were right where she had seen them on her way out that morning. I stood there feeling like a fool realizing that she had lied to me so I would take the wrong trail. My people sat around looking kinda disappointed and not saying much. Great way to start a trip.

The next day was just as disappointing. I led my riders up canyon past Upper Pizona Springs, around McNamara Lake, across McBride flat, and over the ridge toward Twin Teats. Nothing! No horses and no tracks. The guests were getting to be whiners and several were not at all comfortable on horseback. Since we hadn't seen horses, they weren't much interested in seeing anything else. The brilliant blue sky, the majestic snow-covered sierra, the miles of sage and pinon, and the mounds of desert apricot covered in pink blossoms were all wasted on them. One woman even cried because it scared her when her horse stepped down off a 6-inch-tall rock. So, I decided to take them a little farther in hopes of finally scaring up some horses. We tried to climb up behind Red Top and instead found a mysterious spot where a winter snow bank had just melted off leaving a very large and very strange bog. It looked just like dry sand but it wasn't. Unfortunately, we found it by riding into it. It got pretty exciting before we all got out safely. By then it was getting late and we were far from home. We were supposed to be back to camp by 4 o'clock as we needed to be ready for dinner by 6 o'clock. We pushed hard and reached camp right at 6 o'clock. My boss, Craig, chewed my butt and told me if I got in later than 4 o'clock the next day, my ass would be grass. Even with all of that my group still hadn't seen one danged horse.

Early the next morning Craig decided to send my group out first in hopes of giving them a shot at finally seeing some horses. Just as we were about to put the riders up on their horses, three guys on dirt bikes blasted through camp and took off up the trail we had planned on using. Needless to say, they beat us to the most likely mustang areas. We rode all the way to Mc Bride without finding any horse tracks that weren't overlaid with dirt bike tracks. Yup, we were screwed.

After a lot of pondering I came up with the thought that there might be another way to find some mustangs. At the head of Horse Trap Canyon there was a swale that led off up the hill to the west. It headed toward an area where we didn't usually travel, but on second thought whenever there was a disturbance in those more used areas there seemed to be quite a few fresh tracks heading off up that swale. I had never trailed them out, but it seemed like a good bet today.

I explained to my riders that we would try to follow an old wagon road north out of McBride, then pick up a horse trail across the top of the ridge which would drop us down to the head of Horse Trap. I had cut across from Horse Trap to McBride many times, but this would be the first time I had tried to back-track it. Seemed like a good idea at the time.

One good thing I noticed at this time was that my riders, mostly gals, seemed a lot surer of themselves than they had been just the day before. None of them complained or even hesitated. They just nodded and rode on. Too bad they didn't have a guide worthy of them. Because, guess what? We were in trouble again. I had never realized before that there were two wagon roads coming out of that section of McBride. And, of course, we were on the wrong one.

The turnoff we were seeking was marked by a horse trail swinging off to the left, up a curved ridge, and through a burned-off area. Hard to miss a spot like that, but I just couldn't find it. So, we just kept riding and I just kept desperately looking for the turn off while trying to pretend that I knew exactly where we were going.

Eventually we topped a ridge and, in the distance, I could see a valley. With sinking heart, I stared at a completely barren alkali valley that I knew that I had never seen before. I just stopped the whole group and rode to the back of the line where a packer named Wes was leading the pack mule and bringing up the drag. I rode up next to him and speaking softly so as not to upset the guests I asked him if he had any idea where the hell we were. What I didn't realize was that he was fast asleep in the saddle and that my little question woke him up.

He jerked upright in his saddle staring wildly at that barren grey and white valley, and hollered at the top of his lungs, "Hontoon Valley! By God, that's Hontoon Valley. That's where all the wild burro herds are. I've never actually seen it before. Well, I'll be darned, Hontoon Valley!"

Well, so much for not letting our guests know we were in trouble. At that point, I just sat there on good old Abby mule and looked all around us hoping for some kinda inspiration. Pretty soon it occurred to my dust clogged brain that the shallow canyon below us led off to our left and then up a long dry meadow to a ridge top that looked a lot like the area above the head of Horse Trap Canyon.

First, we had to get down into the little canyon. The canyon itself had a wide, smooth, sandy bottom, but getting down to it looked like it might be a bit tough. It was sorta steep and involved working our way down through a jumble of sage brush and volcanic boulders. I told my gals that I would ride down to the bottom then they could come down to meet me. I gave them their choice of riding down, getting off and leading their animals down, or just cutting their horses lose and walking down. While I rode down, Wes helped those who needed help to get off and to tie up the reins on the ones who were turning lose. Wes would push any lose stock and I would catch up at the bottom. Looked a little chaotic, but worked just fine. Pretty soon we were all back in the saddle and drifting on up that canyon. These gals were starting to look like hands.

After an easy ride up the canyon and across the dry meadow, we came to the swale above Horse Trap that we had been looking for in the first place. And as I had originally guessed, it held the fresh tracks of about a dozen mustangs. My idea that we wanted to go there was good, but my execution was pretty poor. I congratulated my people on finding where the mustangs had gone to hide from the dirt bikes. Unfortunately, it was now too late in the day to follow those tracks. We were barely going to make it back to camp in time for dinner and that was just about two hours later than the deadline Craig had impressed on me the night before.

Riding down Horse Trap Canyon most of the trail is an old mustang trail washed out by the winter rains to make a long V shaped depression in the sand. The flats around us were mostly black sage and being down in the V our horses' backs were about level with the sandy surface of the flats. Ridin' along in the lead, I was mostly concentrating on keeping the group moving at a fast walk, hoping that the boss wouldn't actually fire me, and regretting bitterly that I hadn't found these folks some horses. After what must have been a pretty tough day for them, there was no grousing back there, just mostly talking and even some giggling.

After a while the girl in the black crash helmet who was riding right behind me said, "Hey, Irene, if we were to see a cat up here, what would it be?"

"Well, do you mean a domestic cat or a wild one?"

"Wild," she said.

"Well, was it solid or spotted?"

"Solid," she said.

"Hmmm, was it big or little?"

"Big," she said.

"Did it have a long tail or a short tail?"

"It had a long tail," she said.

"Dang, that's a mountain lion. When the heck did you see that?" I asked thinking that it must have been somewhere near camp yesterday.

"Oh," she said, "I saw it just now when it ran across the trail between your mule and my horse."

I whipped Abby around stopping the whole group and yelled something intelligent like, "What!"

The two gals behind her had seen the mountain lion too. We checked the tracks and saw that he had kept right on going. I started to ask Wes if he had seen it, but he had been asleep again and missed it.

Well, we kept on going, too, right on into camp and just in time for dinner. The boss was kind enough not to fire my ass.

After dinner we all gathered around the campfire. The groups were sitting on opposite sides of the fire. I was standing by my group drinking a cup of coffee and wishing it was something stronger. Pretty soon the-other-guide asked me if we had seen any horses. Adding that, of course, their group had seen horses.

I kinda hung my head in shame and admitted that we hadn't. Surprised that they had seen anything with the dirt bikes around, I asked where they had seen them. She answered that they hadn't seen any since the first day but that was sure more than we had seen. I kinda nodded my head and allowed as how that was true.

Just then I heard a sound behind me and looked around. My whole group had gotten out of their chairs and were standing in a solid line beside me. The girl in the black crash helmet stepped forward and growled, "Horses! We don't need to see no stinkin' horses! You should have been where we were!" And pretty soon they were jumping up and down, and laughing, and slapping each other on the back while they told everyone there about the mountain lion, and Hontoon Valley, and the snow bog, and Horse Trap Canyon, and finding the tracks in the swale, and turning the horses lose down the canyon, and Wes being asleep leading the mule.

This hilarity went on well into the night. Eventually Wes showed up to dance around the fire wearing his brown Mongolian robe and three-wolf-tails hat. And a good time was had by all. And I had to spend a little time ponderin' on how I had misjudged my team of riders. They had sure turned out to be something special. And I had to agree that they really didn't need no stinkin' horses.

RIDIN' FENCE AT THE POOL FIELD

So did you ever wonder where the horses and mules go in the winter time when the whole sierra sleeps under ten or twenty feet of snow? Unlike your other summer stuff you can't just throw them behind the seat in the pickup till next packing season. A few animals work in warm areas like Death Valley or are leased out to give riding lessons at various schools. However, most of them are turned out to pasture to rest and recuperate from the hard summer's work. Most of the stock from Rock Creek Pack Trains winter in the Pool Field on the floor of Owens Valley about five miles northeast of Independence.

The Pool Field is a 6,000-acre field leased from LADWP by three of the High Sierra Pack outfits: Rock Creek, Reds Meadows, and Mammoth Lakes. Those outfits keep a combined total of 200 to 300 head of stock there in the winter. The land varies from sand and sage to bunch grass and willows. It stretches from the aqueduct clear across the valley to the base of the Inyo Mountains. DWP releases flood irrigation water onto the field in places, in amounts and at times which seem to be completely unpredictable, at least to those of us who have to work there. Often when checking the fences or looking over the stock, the trail you took last week turns out to be under three feet of water this week. Ah, the packing business, always an adventure.

Incidentally, the Pool Field is not named for these ever moving pools of water, but for the fact that three outfits pool their stock together there. Riding fence there is done at least once a week and involves riding all the way around the outside edge, checking and repairing any fence damage, closing any gates that have been left open, and checking for any tracks going out an open gate or down fence. In addition, you find and count as many head of stock as you can. While doing that you check over the stock for injuries, illnesses, or major weight loss. Any animal that is hurt or sick gets moved to the boss's place in Bishop. Since the boss is a vet, that makes sense. Any animal losing weight gets moved to the Diaz Lake field in Lone Pine where they get extra hay and care.

The first time I actually rode fence on the Pool Field was a real eye opener. Over the years I had been to that field a number of times to gather stock, get ready for the horse drive, or to return escaped animals. Strangely enough, whenever you mentioned the east side fence the guys always did that thing where they slide looks at each other and snicker. They would never say what that was all about, so the first time I was sent to ride the entire perimeter, I asked Dr. London if there was anything I should know about the east fence. He just said that I would know when I saw it. Great!!

Well, I saw it. It's about 12 miles around the field. I started at the catch pens and went down the aqueduct fence to the south fence. Then I followed the south fence east about five miles across three dirt roads, one set of big power lines, the dried-up river bed, and the old railroad right-of-way. Finally, as I started to work my way into the jumbled rocks of the eastern foothills, I realized that the joke was on me as usual. There was no eastern fence line. It was just rough enough and far enough from water and feed that someone had figured that none of the horses would bother to go out that way. So, when the abandoned train tracks and the fences with them were torn out in the 50's no one bothered to replace the fence. Worked pretty good until they got a captured mustang named Red who was responsible for several escapes that way. Still I guess the outfit figured it was easier to round up Red and his buddies each spring than to build two miles of fence through the rocks.

Riding the Pool Field was almost always an education. You learned that nothing grew under the salt cedar because it dripped salt onto the ground around it so it never had to compete with other plants. You were alone in the open enough that you got where you could actually see the weather patterns as they formed over the valley. You found the remains of old horses that hadn't survived the last winter. Often there was enough hide left to identify color, marking and sometimes brands. I would always jot those down in my notebook to pass on to the bosses so they could get some idea of what animals they might have lost.

One time I came upon a carcass by the water gate near the catch pens. The local scavengers were still working on it. As I rode by, three coyotes, two golden eagles, several ravens, and half a dozen magpies were at work. I figured when I had finished circling the field in about four hours, I would come back and take a closer look. When I got back, they were pretty much done with him. Looking at his color and markings I realized that he was a small chestnut gelding from Rock Creek named Pacer. He was quite elderly and his death wasn't a total surprise. What was a surprise was that his remains looked just like other remains that I had assumed were months or even years old. Since it was only a week since I had seen him alive and well, it seemed that nature was cleaning up the equine remains with much greater speed and efficiency than I had ever imagined. It's this kind of ponderin' that keeps you from tearin' up when you find an old friend like Pacer who has gone on to the next great pasture.

One of the messiest adventures Abby and I ever had in the Pool Field had to do with the boys from DWP moving the water and the amazing weather we have here on the lee side of the Sierras. I trailered my riding mule, Abby, to the field fairly early that morning as the weather seemed like it might turn a tad nasty as the day went on. Well, I saddled up and we headed out into the field. The first two things I noticed were that I could see the little black dots that were livestock off to the northeast along the north fence, and also that most of the area between us and them was filled with new ponds and swamps created by a recent flood irrigation. Normally, we would have ridden the fence around the entire field coming back through that area where the stock was. But the weather looked like it might make it a good idea to cut our visit short this fine morning.

On this particular day I could see the leading edge of a rainstorm coming over the Sierras and heading due east toward where we were riding. You could see a dark gray line of rain sweeping down the foothills and across the valley. At the same time there was a whole different storm coming out of the south. It was a windstorm carrying a wall of alkali dust off the dry lake south of Lone Pine and heading it north up the valley. Since it looked like we were surrounded, I decided that that most useful thing we could do was to get close enough to the horses to make a quick head count and then start back to the truck and trailer.

We started off working our way across all the new water hazards. Some were just shallow streams we could walk across. Then there were many that were deep muddy bogs, rafts of tules, and other deep holes that the mule could barely struggle across. Mules have a lot harder time with this kind of terrain than horses. Horse hooves are fairly wide and flat whereas mule's hooves are small and pointy. When you get a mule into deep mud his feet just drive right into it and stick. Abby and I plunged into muddy hole after muddy hole, struggling and thrashing our way out of one just to come across another. Of course, in the back of my mind were the tales of riders coming off their mount in such a situation, getting caught under the struggling animal, and getting beat to death by the animal's threshing hooves. All that meant was that I was holdin' on tight. Looking around the field at all the open lonesome country around us and at the ugly storms moving our way, I figured that if we managed to get into real trouble, it might take a day or two until anyone found us. Finally, we came to a place where we were only one more hole away from dry land and the horses we were looking for. The minute we stepped in I knew we were in trouble. It was a good foot of gray alkali mud topped by enough water to reach to the seat of my saddle. Abby fought like a mountain lion, but my weight and the deep water and mud were more than she could handle. When she finally gave out and quit struggling, I slipped off her side and into the water. A little struggling of my own and a lot of luck, and I made it onto the bank of the hole. I was still holding Abby's reins so I went to pullin' on her. With my weight off her back and a little help from my pullin', she managed to work her hooves free of the mud and scramble out of the hole. For the first few minutes we just leaned on each other and trembled. That was a close one.

When we both quit shaking, I got back on and we rode to the big herd. A fast count gave us about 220 head which was close enough to what was supposed to be there to assume that it was likely no one had escaped or been stolen. Choosing a longer but drier route, we headed back to the truck and trailer. Riding along and hoping that we wouldn't run into anyone we knew on the way home, I took stock of our appearance. We were pretty much covered in gray mud, me from my waist down, and Abby everywhere except her head and neck. I had been kinda worried about that rainstorm catching up with us, but now I was hoping that it would. I figured we couldn't look worse and it might wash some of the mud off. No such luck. Just before we reached the rig, the weather caught us. But it wasn't a nice clean rain. Instead, the dust storm from the south met the rain storm from the west right over our heads. The alkali dust mixed with the rain and fell as big drops of gray mud, covering all those parts of Abby and I that weren't already mud covered. Of course, it also covered the truck and trailer.

So, we loaded up and headed out, now really hoping that we would be unobserved on our way home. I know guys with lots of money like to match their truck and trailer, but this probably the first time anyone had seen a rider, mule, saddle, truck and trailer that were all the same exact shade of gray. Purty fancy, alright.

UH, NO, I DON'T SPEAK JAPANESE. DOES IT MATTER?

Many trips in the "High Lonesome" require things of the crew that you never imagined in your wildest dreams. Riding through the wilderness for seven days on a mule that had never been ridden before... Crossing a 12,000 foot pass alone in a "whiteout" blizzard trusting to your mule to find the way... Getting your chinks covered in blood as you walked an injured guest out of the "Rough" above Bridgeport... Sleeping next to the food every night to guard it from the bears...But one of the most difficult challenges was nine days on the long loop from Mono to Pine Creek leading a group of Japanese who essentially spoke no English.

So, we're talking about a group of ten or so Japanese business people, all inexperienced on horses and mules. This was a private, all expense trip. That means the itinerary, length of moves, and menu were all set by the guests. That makes many things different from the average trip. One of the guests on this trip was the author of the book that was considered the definitive Japanese text on the life of John Muir. Since he was considered an expert, this man had planned the route (much of which was on the John Muir trail), the stops, and the menu. See, that lets me blame most of the problems on the trip on him. Right. And of course, there were going to be problems.

Getting ready for the trip was a lot of extra work, and the night before the trip we met our guests for dinner in town at Whiskey Creek.

They came in a big van accompanied by a driver who was also their interpreter. It was a great dinner and afterwards one of the local store owners opened up his western wear store so our visitors could outfit themselves in western wear. Things looked real promising.

The next morning, they met us at the pack station for breakfast. Our packers, Gerald, Little Phil, and Scotty packed up their loads while Irene (that's me, the little old pack cook and guide), with the help of station crew put the new riders up on their equines. While doing that, out of the corner of my eye I saw their van driver (and only interpreter) get in the van and drive away. And he kept on going down the road and away. With a sinking feeling, I asked the boss if that was going to be a problem. He said not to worry as one of the other guests, the owner of the travel agency which had planned this trip, would be our translator. Going back to putting guests up on horses, I soon found myself working with the travel agent. As I was adjusting his stirrup leathers, he asked me in rather broken English how we could be sure that the guests stayed in their saddles. Thinking he spoke English, I made a wise crack about gluing their jeans to the saddles. Thirty minutes later I was still unsuccessfully trying to explain what glue was and I knew we were in big trouble if we needed something translated.

Before long, we had all our riders up and started out up the Mono Pass trail. As was usual with good dude stock, the riders just sat there while the animals lined out walking quietly up the trail. Scotty rode drag, following behind the group prepared to give help if anyone got in trouble. It went fine until we came to the Ruby Lake turnoff at the bottom of the sandy switchbacks. Most of our day rides used this spot for a lunch stop or as the turn-around for short rides. With no real direction from their riders, our animals decided they could do anything they pleased. Some wandered off, some turned back, some just went to grazing. Scotty was yelling directions to the riders which isn't very useful if your riders don't speak English. It looked a whole lot like that commercial where they're herding cats. One rider was a 73-year-old lady who had never ridden anything before. Her mule just wandered off and she was completely terrified. I rode up to her and caught her mule's lead rope. Actually, that was how we rode for the entire remainder of the trip. We started up the switchbacks and Scotty herded the rest of them onto the trail behind us. Scotty is one of those extremely conscientious people and he was desperately trying to shout instructions to our inexperienced, non-English-speaking people. He was looking pretty desperate and I sorta thought he might be crying in frustration. It took two extra hours to reach that night's camp.

That night after the guests had wandered off to bed, we had a little crew conference around the dying campfire. It seemed plain that language was going to be a problem. Most of our guests spoke only Japanese. The only two who actually spoke English refused to translate. The author who had organized the trip was a celebrity and felt it was beneath him to translate for the crew as we were essentially servants. Saeko, a business woman from Tokyo, would not translate as the men in the group would not stand for having a woman give them instructions. My riding friend spoke no English except by the end of the trip she knew, "straighten your saddle, lean back, and look up," the three things she needed to do to stay on her mule. The third woman was really sad. She never spoke at all. I actually wondered if she even spoke Japanese.

Fortunately, our next day's move was only about four easy miles down canyon. All but one of our guests and my riding lady were going to hike and the Muir expert would guide them. So, we didn't need any riding lesson that morning. Oh, the one rider? That was the man with the broken ankle. Yup, we actually had a guest riding with his ankle in a cast. Anyway, that was a relatively easy day and the guests were thrilled because we were now actually on the John Muir Trail.

So, we had a pleasant evening at Quail Meadow, a nice little camp near where Mono Creek crossed the JMT. Immediately after breakfast the next morning, we gathered around the campfire for our riding lesson. Saeko volunteered to help me. She pretended to be the riding animal (mule or horse as necessary). I hung a bridle on her head and demonstrated the difference between neck reining a horse and straight reining a mule. We acted out long-eared mules and short-eared horses. Saeko translated some necessary parts and my pantomime was apparently highly amusing. Laughter doesn't require much translation. Then we got everyone on their animals. Leading my old lady's mule, Lolly, we started up the endless switchbacks of Bear Ridge. It was a long day, about seventeen miles, but everyone made it to our next camp on Bear Creek.

The following day on Bear Creek was the only layover day of this little sojourn in the wilderness. It was a day filled with many surprises. It turned out to be Saeko's birthday. Therefore, I had to rearrange the menu so I could bake a birthday cake for dinner. Saeko had been such a great help on this trip that I decided I should have a birthday present for her. I dug through my duffle and found a new handkerchief scarf that I had just bought recently. I wrapped it in foil, string and little pinecones. Sometimes you got to be a bit creative.

Another interesting moment was around noon when I discovered that Japanese men are much like the French and German guests I have traveled with in that they like to swim in the creeks and that they don't really care to wear anything while they do it. So, I was doing some cooking and the wide spot in the creek was right next to camp. So, I guess you could say I was cookin' and lookin' right then. Japanese men are pretty much slender and in good shape. It was a fine sight, especially there was one guy with his back to me who was definitely fine. He wasn't quite as tan as the rest of the guys but that was one eye-catching body. I turned away, afraid they might turn around and catch me lookin'. After a while "Mr. Eye Candy" turned around and much to my surprise, it was Scotty, my drag rider. Since Scotty was a fireman the rest of the year, it shouldn't have been a surprise that he was in great shape, but I never did have the guts to tell him that I had been peeking.

The day ended with a birthday party for Saeko and the following morning saw us back on the trail This day we would leave Bear Creek, travel upcreek to Rosemarie, cross Selden Pass, and drop into the valley of the San Joaquin where we would take the lower trail so we could drop off to a campsite near the hot spring above Shooting Star. It's a hard camp to locate so I was happy to hear Gerald telling the boss that he knew how to find it. Since we would not get there until afternoon, the pack strings would be ahead of the riders That meant we needed to have a packer who could locate the camp.

On this particular day about half of our guests were hiking and the other half rode. Of course, I was once more leading Lolly mule and her inexperienced rider. Coming over the pass we got a pretty heavy rain, but it didn't last too long. Half way down the pass Gerald and Little Phil passed us with the strings. We stopped for lunch at the Twin Lakes and were passed by most of our hikers. Fortunately, I had asked them to wait for us at the trail fork at the bottom of the canyon. So, we reached the junction with the low trail and picked up our hikers. Together with all our guests, we started up canyon on the low trail following our packers' mule tracks. Within the next 100 feet we should have turned off to cross the meadow to the river. Unfortunately, the mule tracks didn't turn off. So, we kept following them. Maybe Gerald was going to use a different trail. About a mile later, I figured maybe Gerald knew a different camp. The tracks kept going so so did we. Another mile or so and we were still following uphill mule tracks. After a while I stopped some hikers and asked them if they had seen the mules. They had and they identified them as wearing tarps that said Rock Creek on them. Yes, they were our packers and they were still going. By this time, I had switched all the "maybes" to one "certain" and that was that Gerald was a damn liar and didn't have a clue where we were going. Not long after that we hit the point where the low trail rejoined the high trail. I knew that there were no more camping spots above there for many miles. So, I helped Scotty tie up our stock off the trail and left him with all our guests while Abby and I took off in pursuit of our wandering packers. As I took a last glance back at our party waiting by the trail, I was less than pleased to notice a rather magnificent sunset taking place behind us. Not a good sign. Gettin' a little late.

One of the great things about my mule Abigail was that before I bought her she had competed in endurance races. So, I put her off at a high trot and we covered a lot of ground pretty quickly. My big worry was that only a mile or two ahead of us the trail split. To the right it crossed a big bridge and entered the park in some pretty rough country. We needed to turn left on Paiute Creek, but we didn't want to do it tonight as it was several miles of steep, rocky cliffs high above the creek with no place to stop. Fortunately, I caught up with the boys right at the bridge. Gerald's mules had refused to cross the bridge which gave me time enough to catch up with them. Using some pretty unpleasant language, I urged the strings and their packers off the bridge and quickly back down canyon.

It only took me a few minutes to convince our celebrity leader that we should camp where we were instead of going back down canyon to our original campsite. I made a quick dinner of stir fry and rice which the exhausted guests gobbled down and soon I was doing dishes in the dark. Earlier I had worried about that meal as our celebrity leader had demanded that I remove all rice dishes from my menu since they weren't western enough for our cowboy trip. This was the only one remaining and I expected him to gripe about it. It would have been a fitting ending to a hard day, however he never said a word. Later most of the guests were gathered around a nice campfire near the river. I was searching for a missing pot so I could finish up the dishes. Eventually I discovered that the three ladies had swiped the pan and were gathered around it out in the meadow where they were carefully picking out and eating every remaining grain of rice. Guess our leader slightly misjudged their taste for rice.

Sure hoped the next day would be a bit less challenging. We would all be on horseback as it was a pretty steep haul. At least this time it was Little Phil who knew where the campsite was as he used to work for Pine Creek, the outfit that rode this area most often.

The next morning, we spent a few minutes with a trail map making sure that we all knew where the Merriam camp was. Then we were off and up Paiute Creek. It rained again but this time it was long and serious. We struggled and scrambled up the rugged trail along steep cliffs far above the raging creek. When we finally reached the first level spot, we crossed through a barbed wire drift fence and tied up to stop for lunch. As we ate, we watched our strings come through the gate and move on ahead of us up the trail. I was suddenly reminded of the time not too many years before when another pack train had lost an entire string when the creek swept them away at that very spot. Keeping that in mind made our trip's problems seem pretty minor.

Soon we were done with lunch and on our way again. Scotty was riding lead and Lolly and her rider were with me riding drag. It had quit raining for a while, but started up again just before we got to Hutchinson Meadow, where the trail split again. At this point in a rather spectacular grove of Jeffery pines the trail split into a right branch leading over Paiute Pass to North Lake and a left branch leading to our next camp sited below the Merriam waterfall. As soon as Scotty reached the trail junction, I heard him holler.

"Hey, Irene, you need to come up here."

"What's wrong?" I asked.

All he said was, "We've got tracks up here."

"Well, I should hope so since the strings are ahead of us."

"Come and look!" he yelled.

So, I did and sure enough, there were the tracks of 10 mules and 2 horses turning right at the junction and heading off towards Paiute Pass. After a quick check to make sure there were no other tracks on the left trail, I gave Lolly's lead rope to Scotty and took off one more time in pursuit of our lost boys. Now I needed to kill Gerald AND Little Phil. Seems like it took about an hour to catch up with them, or maybe more. When I finally found them, they were clear up on the pass. When Phil heard me coming behind them, he turned and saw us coming fast and just said, "Oh.no. Not again!" Instead of being sympathetic and remembering how it feels when you are the one who took a wrong turn, I just started yelling at them. Phil called me over and reminded me that Gerald had done time for hurting an old lady who gave him a hard time. It seemed he thought that I should quit yelling. So, I did.

On the way back to the junction I got a chance to point out Pilot's Knob, a big white bluff that marked our junction. Getting there I expected to find all our people huddled and unhappy in the rain. Instead, Scotty had used the opportunity to teach all our guests how to build their own campfires. So, there they stood warm and proud of their accomplishments.

So then Scotty taught them how to safely put their fires out and we rode on to our campsite. Merriam is a spectacular site where an optical illusion makes it appear that a waterfall comes straight out of the top of a mountain. The rain had stopped and the scattered clouds broke into pinks and golds as the sun lowered. As we started to unpack and set up camp, I told the packers that dinner was a leg of lamb that would take quite a bit of time to prepare and that it might be a good idea to plan something to entertain our guests. Dinner did take quite a while as the only good way to prepare lamb in camp is to bone it out, butterfly it, marinate it, and grill it over the coals. Meanwhile the packers came up with a brilliant idea. They built some dummies out of chairs, coats, and hats and then taught our guests how to rope. I mean "genuwine", out-on-the-range roping. They learned and they were thrilled.

Now the only person on the trip who wasn't happy was the poor Okinawan lady. She seemed all alone, didn't speak English, and none of the Japanese guests seemed to speak to her. Sitting by the fire where

I was grilling the lamb, she spoke softly. It wasn't either English or Japanese, but Scotty who was nearby leaped to his feet as if he had been goosed with a fire poker. Scotty, being a fireman in San Diego, of course, spoke Spanish and that was what she had spoken. He sat down next to her and asked her a question. Well, that was it. They didn't stop chatting until well after dinner and campfire were over. Scotty was thrilled to be such a source of pleasure to the sad lady, and she looked happier than I had ever seen anyone look. It was a great last night for what had been a purty rough trip.

Only one more day left. We would ride up French Canyon, top over the pass, work our way through the lakes, hikers, and campers, and come out on the canyon wall. Then we would work our way down the brushy, dusty switchbacks to Pine Creek Pack Station on the floor of the canyon where we would hand our guests back to their van and interpreter. At this point on many trips the crew would be looking forward some tips, but we had been informed well ahead of this trip that the Japanese do not tip. Guess it's a cultural thing. As difficult as this trip had been, looking forward to the end of it was probably enough of a reward.

So, we went on as we had started, Scotty leading and me with the old lady on Lolly bringing up the drag. In front of us was the most serious guest on our slowest mule, Maxine. Sick of dragging behind a mule who was only going slow cause she thought she had her rider's number, I hollered at him to kick her up. He made a serious try but she just ignored him. Losing my temper, I rode up behind Maxine and popped her in the rump with my lead rope. Just as my rope hit her, it occurred to me that that might not be a real smart idea. She took off at a high trot and I held my breath hoping the old man wouldn't fall off. He went with her, holding on and yelling, "Yahoo!" He looked around and gave me a huge grin. Guess he liked it.

Not too much later, Scotty rode back to us and offered to lead Lolly for a while as I had been doing it for 9 days. I refused but he insisted and I took the lead. Guess my "keeping the old lady on the mule instructions" were not good enough because within about 10 minutes she came crashing off the mule to land in a pile of rocks. Fortunately, she wasn't hurt and I resumed my mule-leading post.

Now that Maxine was keeping up, my little group at the back were getting left behind. Lolly was being slow and careful down the steep rocks, Abby was hurrying to keep up with Maxine and my arms were getting stretched out between them. Keeping Lolly's rider safe was most important, so I bailed off Abby and turned her lose. Then I walked and led Lolly for the last three miles or so. It was hot and dusty and, of course, I was feeling sorry for myself.

Riding into the pack station I could see that everyone else was already there and off their animals. I was sweaty and dusty. My rider was looking pretty wore out, but she was still there on that mule. It occurred to me that she should be damn proud of herself. Out of sight of the others, I stopped our little group for a few minutes. Using mostly gestures and a few words, I convinced her that we should enter the station yard tall and proud. When we came into their sight, she was tall, straight on the mule, and sporting a huge grin. They all ran over and congratulated her. It was a great moment.

Later the people who don't tip gave us numerous gifts, scarves, autographed fans, and the rider on Maxine even gave me his watch. Then they piled into the van and as they started to drive off, I realized that despite everything, I would miss them. Then the van made a sudden stop and quickly backed up to where the crew was standing. The side door slid open and my long-term riding partner leaped out. She ran to me and threw herself into my arms. In broken English she stammered, "So sad... never see you again... love you..." Then, crying, she kissed me on the cheek and ran back to the van. I waved as the van pulled away again and realized that my eyes were a little damp too.

FOREST FIRE

Not all the fires in my life were in the middle of a campsite. Occasionally the campsite was in the middle of a fire. For thirteen years of my life I was married to a fire fighter for the Forest Service. With my background as a camp cook and that connection with the USFS it was inevitable that I would end up working some forest service spike camps on some forest fires. The most memorable of those was one June up on the Shepard Pass trail. The fire was a lightning-caused spot fire at the 11,000-foot level on the north face of Mount Williamson. Often fires at that elevation are left to burn themselves out, but in this case some of the burning trees burned all the way through, fell, and rolled in a flaming mass all the way to the bottom of the canyon. When they landed in the riparian zone along the creek at the 7,000-foot level, they would of course light it off, too.

This kind of fire normally calls for the use of helicopters; to haul in fallers to chainsaw the burning trees before they can roll, to spot in hotshot teams in the riparian zone, to make water drops on anything that is burning. Unfortunately, the winds during this fire were so strong that you didn't dare to get a chopper in the air. So, they had to hike the fire crews in on foot. The fire camp and supplies had to be brought in on mule trains.

By the time I became involved, the fire had been burning for two days. The crews were in a camp.at the 10,000-foot level. They had to hike from the camp down into the canyon then up the other side to

11,000 feet to work on the fire. They were sleeping in paper sleeping bags and eating leftover military rations (gut packs) from the Vietnam era. Weather reports made it obvious that continuing high winds would keep the fire crews without air support for another five or six days. The District Ranger in Lone Pine decided that a mountain cook, some camp equipment, and fresh food would do a lot toward improving the firemen's lives. So, at 3 AM I woke up to a message on the Forest Net radio. By 5 AM I was at the grocery store in Lone Pine which had opened four hours early just for us. Not too much later with the help of a couple of USFS people, I had four huge baskets full of food and was headed for the trail head at Symmes Creek. There I met a packer and string from Onion Valley. We climbed up the Shepherd Pass trail on what seemed like an infinite number of switchbacks and eventually topped over into the next canyon to the south. Within a couple hundred yards the ridge widened into a hogback where the fire camp was situated.

It was late afternoon and the camp was empty. The packer unloaded the camp supplies and all the fresh food, hauled five-gallon tins of water from the nearest creek, then loaded up all his empty pack equipment and hit the trail home. The wind was howling down the canyon but I could make out the smoke high above me from the original fire and several spot fires. It was the middle of June but that wind was colder than snake snot. I knew that up that mountain I had thirty or so fire fighters who would come dragging into camp sometime after dark; dirty, exhausted, and about three-days-worth of hungry.

What I had brought with me was everything I found in the store that I thought they might want. I was instructed to bring a 24-hour supply and to be prepared to radio in another day's order right after breakfast the next morning. My supply officer would pick up everything on the list and send it up on mules the next afternoon. As far as I can remember that first night's dinner was really big steaks, corn on the cob, potato salad, garlic bread, baked beans, green salad, and watermelon. I also discovered that my supply officer had added five apple pies and four bottles of wine, just because...

It was just after dark and dinner was ready. The wind was still howling, but it was colder now and spitting snow. Eventually the fire fighters returned to camp. They staggered in a few at a time dragging their tools behind them. They were so covered in soot that at first all you could see in the dark was their eyes. They sorta washed up, wolfed down everything in sight while making little grunts of gratitude, and hurried off to their paper sleeping bags to try for some well-earned rest. While I did up the dishes, the head of the Mammoth Hotshots dug a fair-sized trench in the sand right beside the camp. Then he got out my sleeping bag and spread it in the trench. He explained that that would break the wind so maybe I could get warm enough to sleep. Damned thoughtful coming from a guy who had just put in a 28-hour day.

So, for the next six days I lived on the hogbacked ridge that separates Symmes Creek Canyon from the lower reaches of Shepherd Creek. We were living on the sandy ridge among the manzanita and wind-twisted pines. Far below us Shepherd Creek crashed its way through a completely impassable rock chute to the valley floor. To our south the north face of Mt Williamson loomed over us. High above us on the 11,000-foot level of that face was where our hotshots were fighting the fire. The wind continued to howl day and night for the next six days.

During those six days I radioed out an order for food daily and it came to us on a string of mules. It always seemed to contain a few items that I hadn't ordered, usually bottles of wine. My supply officer was a local boy who had grown up in his folks' bar and seemed to think that guys who worked as hard as my crews needed a little after dinner cheer. I'm sure it was completely against the USFS rules, but nobody said anything. It reached the point where some of the firemen were critiquing the wines as they were passed around the evening campfire. Something Thurberesk like "This is a frisky little zinfandel, with notes of pine and undertones of woodsmoke and manzanita berries." It was very funny at the time.

The most memorable incident on this trip to the wilderness happened sometime around the second night there. Dinner was over and the exhausted firefighters were sprawled around the campfire prior to dragging themselves off to bed. Like I mentioned before, they were so smoke blackened that they looked like hulking black shapes with only their eyeballs glowing in the dark. Suddenly one of the guys leaped to his feet and hollered, "Shit! It's a spot fire." He was pointing along the ridge to the east. And sure enough, about 200 feet away was the glow of a small fire. Seven or eight of the guys leaped to their feet, grabbed their shovels, and sprinted down the ridge toward the spot. Soon you could hear yells and see dark leaping shapes looming in the light of the little fire. In just moments, the fire was out and you could hear the sounds of digging as they buried the coals. Pretty soon the guys returned to camp and for having put it out so quickly they seemed kinda down. They had sounded pretty enthusiastic while actually putting it out, lots of yelling and running around. A couple of guys said they had stomped it out. Another two said they shoveled dirt on it. One even admitted he had peed on it to make sure it was out. I commented that they didn't seem real pleased about it and their leader said that the two backpackers who had been cooking their dinner over that fire weren't real pleased either. I shouldn't have laughed, but damn it was funny.

In a few days the boys got a handle on the main fire and the Mammoth Hotshots were sent home. The seven guys from the Deadman Slash Crew stayed to clean up any hotspots. On the sixth day the winds finally laid down and they got the chopper in the air. The pilot brought it in to check the camp for a landing spot. He radioed me that I would be coming out on horseback the next day and they would work the fire from the air after that. It happened to be my birthday and I was feeling a little neglected and ready to go home. I always was an emotional "baby." Just before Pat, the pilot, took his helicopter back to base, he hovered ten feet over my camp and sang Happy Birthday to me over the Forest Net radio. Against the rules but it absolutely tickled me to death.

The next day the pack strings arrived to pull out most of the camp and haul the equipment and the old cook down the mountain. After the long ride down the Symmes Creek trail, my left knee was so swollen I could barely walk. The soft pad below and outside of the kneecap was puffed up enough to push the knee cap clear out of place. This wasn't the first time my knee had done this, and it had reached the point that I figured I was about finished riding livestock and working in the packing business. Yesterday's birthday was pretty close to thirty and there weren't a lot of old people in the packing game. Best present I ever got was that day when the packer, a guy I'd never seen before, walked over to me and asked, "Knee bothering you?" Trying to kid about it I allowed as how it was an old football injury from high school. Ignoring my smart mouth, he explained that I was locking out my knee on the downhill and if I would just raise my heel a little and concentrate on softening my knee, it would get better. By golly he was right! Now, 40 years later, I am still riding the high country. Many parts of my body are pretty shot, but that left knee still actually works. That was some of the best advice I ever got, second only to when Anne Scott taught me to eat mustard for leg cramps. Private joke. Ask me about it the next time I see you.

GUESS WHO I MET ON THE TRAIL

As I looked back over my many years on the trails of the High Sierra, someone asked me why I never talk about the people I met on those trails. Many times, it's because it was a thoroughly unpleasant meeting. Most times though it is a simple case of stopping, explaining to the hikers the safest way for us to pass each other, and then moving on. By the way there are some safety rules for these passing on the trail moments. The first rule is that the stock party has the right of way. This is simply because it's safer that way. First you stop your party. Then you ask the hikers to clear the trail. You ask them to all get on the same side of the trail so if a mule spooks away from a hiker, it won't land on a hiker on the other side. If you are on a steep hillside, you need to get all of them on the downhill side. Why? Because if a hiker is above the mules and he slips or falls, he is likely to slide under the trampling hooves of a thousand-pound mule which could be pretty fatal.

A few other things to mention to the foot traffic include, don't wave your fishing pole around as most equines are dumb enough to think it's a whip and spook at it, if you are in a spot where the animals can't see you, talk loudly so they know you are there, and get far enough off the trail that one of those 100 pound metal side loads can't side-swipe you. If a thousand-pound mule carrying a couple of hundred-pound boxes hits you you're sure to land on your ass.

I kinda like riding in the lead so I can give these little talks to the hikers. Must be a hangover from my school teacher days. Sometimes they like to discuss packing with you which can be fun. Usually I holler, "Heads up" so they will know I'm coming and not be startled by a bunch of big hairy animals looking over their shoulders. Once coming off Shepherd Pass by myself, I was walking and leading my Julie mule because the trail was too steep to ride. Eventually I noticed a hiker ahead of us. We were walking pretty fast so I yelled at him. He ignored me and kept going. Eventually as we walked down the trail, he stopped and sat down on a big rock right in the middle of the trail in front of us. Assuming that something was wrong, I came to a stop about 2 feet behind him. I continued to talk but he just sat there. Eventually, I reached up and tapped him on the shoulder. Boy, did he jump. He whipped around with a terrified look on his face. Then he took a deep breath and tapped his ear. I realized that he was deaf and had no idea that Julie and I were there. We both laughed. He petted Julie on her forehead. And we both continued our way down the trail, Julie and I rapidly outdistancing him.

I remember many times when the hikers were not nearly so nice. One summer I remember leading a party of preteen riders up the Mono Pass trail. Above Ruby Lake we were climbing up the Sandy Switchbacks. That area is tall and nasty. As we reached one of the highest switchbacks, I saw a jogger running down the trail toward us. I was at the rear of the group but I could see ahead of us that he had no intention of being anything but trouble. He ran off the trail along the sandy hillside above our junior riders. As he ran past them, he screamed obscenities at them and kicked rocks down on them and their animals. Fortunately, we had a great group of quiet, steady animals and brave kids. That's one of those times when you wish that karma would drop the guy in the lake below us. No such luck but at least our group all survived.

Another spooky time on the trail was one that Craig London told me about. It seemed he was alone leading a string up out of Island Crossing headed for Red' Meadow. Far, far ahead of him he could see a lone hiker on the same trail. Eventually his glimpses let him know that the hiker was a lone woman. He could see her tracks on the trail ahead of him and he could also see tracks that indicated that some large animal was following her. More tracks and glimpses of the hiker and of something following her lead him to believe that she was being trailed by a mountain lion He was too far away to do anything to help her, but fortunately the lion turned off about ½ mile before they reached Red's.

One of the trail meetings that is really frightening is when you run into some complete nut who for some reason thinks he owns the trails. Once coming off Shepherd Pass at the end of a really long hiker trip I was leading my Abby mule down through the switchbacks which slid with every step you took. That trail had been closed for over 20 years. It was recently reopened but slid all the time and wasn't likely to stay open for too many years. Every time Abby and I took a step we would slide several feet. I don't know how tired she was, but I was about done. At this point I ran into a hiker coming up the right side of the trail. He pulled off to the side and took off his backpack. He yelled about how our animals were destroying the trails and it was against the law for us to be up there. He also said he would file charges with the local police as soon as he got out. I explained to him that we had a written permit from the park service which covered us to the top of the pass and our boss had written permission from the forest service in Lone Pine and the Inyo County Board of Supervisors to cover our travel from the Park line to the floor of the valley. He continued to threaten me and made mention of having a gun and a muttered threat to shoot all of us. By this time, I was too tired to care and didn't figure that a guy standing on moving shale would have a lot of luck hitting me. So, I went on down to our camp and started dinner. I think Craig may have eventually filed charges against the guy but I don't know. Once again, maybe karma got him.

Sometimes the strangest things happen along the trail. Once we were pulling a trip out of Reds Meadows. We were heading down canyon when we ran into two small strings from Reds. We were all three passing each other along a brushy flat. One small string was heading out from the station. The other heading in. They each had 3 or four loads on a small diamond hitch on a small duffle load. The inbound string had what looked like a rough tent pole slid into the outside rope on one side. We had pulled off to the side to allow the other two strings to pass, As they passed each other the pole on one load slid under the ropes of the load passing it. By the time they were through the pole had woven itself into the two loads that were headed opposite directions. By the time they were through, I was holding our string while out packer helped the other two packers get the two strings completely untangled. Sure, the two Reds packers had been hauling the tent post for some reason, but they just pulled it off both loads and threw it in the bushes. Guess we didn't need it either as we also went on without it.

Speaking of strange things, did I ever tell you about the meeting on the trail where Earl mule got his name? Well Earl was a huge black mule, maybe 17 hand tall. In addition to being real tall Earl, like many jacks and johns was seriously well hung. On this occasion one of the Rock Creek packers was leading the big black string in over Mono Pass when he met a group of hikers on the trail near the turn off to Fourth Recess. The hikers were a family group with several small children. After the trip they were on they had pretty much decided to take a riding trip next year and were discussing plans for that trip with the packer. The discussion was long enough that several mules including Earl fell asleep waiting. The little 6-year-old girl spent her time studying the giant black mules standing next to her. Eventually she noticed that as he relaxed, Earl's awesome appendage reached all the way to the ground. When the adults finally quit talking, she tugged on her father's sleeve and yelled, "Look, Daddy, that mule has five legs" Ever after that the big black mule was known as "Earl, the Five Legged Mule."

Sometimes, especially in heavy snow years, the trails end up being blocked at several points and for several reasons. One such year was really memorable. You wouldn't believe what we met on the trail on that trip. To start with the trip was planned to take our hikers in from Mono Pass to the John Muir Trail then north along that trail to come out at Mammoth. Since much of the JMT was snow blocked at several points, we had to work our way around it. The new plan had us coming in over Mono Pass, then by-passing the JMT to continue down canyon past Lake Edison. We were then scheduled to climb up past Graveyard Meadow to the camp at the base of Goodale Pass. We would then layover for a day so the crew could dig a trail through the snow over the pass. Leading out on this section was myself on Julie Mule and a new young packer leading a single string. We were below the snow and it was a beautiful day. Suddenly everything changed. All the trees around us began to buzz. They were alive with deer flies. They are big brown flies that cover you and bite chunks out of you. Julie was in the lead so they swarmed all over her. She was rubbing her face. on the pine trees. It didn't help. I checked with the kid I was packing with but neither of us had any insect repellant. In desperation poor Julie threw herself on the ground. Of course, I ended up on the ground too. I jumped up and began slapping the flies on her face. I killed more than 80 of them on her face. Then I pulled off my wild rag. I used it as a mask on the poor mule and completely covered her face and ears. Luckily, she could see through it. Loud buzzing in the trees told me more deer flies were coming, I guess Julie could hear it, too. She jumped to her feet and I climbed aboard. Since insect swarms like that mainly attack the leader of an animal group, Julie and I dropped to the rear of the mule string. It was only about another two miles to our next camp where we could unpack the mules and get to the RepelX to spray on the animals. What a relief that was for all of us. I really hoped that we wouldn't meet anything more "interesting" during the remaining 12 days of this trip. As usual- wrong guess.

The next day was an easy layover day for myself and the guests. Not so for the Boss and the crew who spent the whole day digging a trail through the snow over Goodale Pass and cutting switchbacks through the deep snow down to Lake of the Lone Indian. Maybe I should throw in a few details on this trip at this point. This was one of the Henkes hiking trips that we took every summer. Originally they had been a group of 20 hikers out for a 15 day trip which was modeled after the Wampler trips of the 1950's. These were the trips that always included a Penny Royal party half way through the trip and had a champagne party on the last lay over day. Gradually over the years the Forest Service and the Park Service limited the size of the trips and at this point we probably had 10 guests in our group. They were still led by Howard Henkes and his wife Petie, but they were by this point both too old to hike the trip. Therefore, they were both learning to ride horses. On each move they were led by a crew member who taught them how to ride their new mode of transportation. This morning of riding the freshly dug trail in the snow our boss, Craig, personally led them over the pass. They were the first ones over the new trail and apparently, they did fine. When I finished tearing down and packing my kitchen, Julie and I got our chance to cross the pass. Even with the excellent job the boys had done the day before, my poor little short legged mule had a fairly hard time hauling the old, fat lady over that trail. Maybe 2/3 of the way down the far side, we got in trouble on the farthest switchback to the left. Julie slipped off the cleared trail and we couldn't get back up on to it. Our only choice was to slip, slide, and wallow our way all the way down to the bottom of the hill. We then buck-jumped our way through the snow to where Craig, Howard, and Petie were waiting at the bottom of the hill. At this point I became the caretaker of our two amateur riders while Craig returned up the pass to help the crew with the remaining strings. As we waited there, a couple of backpackers came along the lower trail from the lake. They stopped in the trail just ahead of us and watched the strings coming off the pass. Pretty soon they were talking nice and loud about how these thoughtless horse packers were destroying the beautiful trail that the Forest Service had cut through the snow for the hikers. They were going on about how the rangers should ticket us. I remember Howard telling me that I should tell them about who dug the trail. After a hard look at them I just told him that there was no point, being as stupid was incurable.

When all the strings were down, we followed them into camp near Grassy Lake. On the way, I realized that every time we jumped down a steep spot Petie would come really close to kitin' off the front of her horse. So, I taught her to lean back and stare at the sky. Every time we'd come to a steep spot, I'd yell at her to look at the sky and she did. Musta worked, because she stayed on pretty good.

Grassy Lake was on a bench high above the south wall of Cascade Valley. Our next move would be further along the bench to Minnow Creek which we would follow until we zig zagged down the steep wall to the meadows of Cascade Valley. Craig had needed to leave our trip at this point so a lot of things were rearranged. I was leading a small string of 3 geriatric mules. The Kid was now in charge of Howard and Petie. While the other strings were still being packed, our little group started out. I noticed that the Kid was doing a pretty good job of helping Petie look at the sky so she wouldn't fall off. After a while we came to the point where creek dropped off the canyon side and we started down the steep switchbacks. We weren't on cliffs but walls and the trees were at pretty similar angles. At one point I noticed the only wide spot anywhere on the trail. Then I turned a corner and looked down at a whole hillside full of people, horses and mules coming up the hill toward us. I was sharing a switchback with a man on horseback leading one pack mule. I let out a hollar and everyone stopped. They were a group of about a dozen private riders. Each of them was riding their own horse and leading one or two pack animals. Farther down the hill, there were places where various riders could pull off the trail. I yelled at Kid to get his riders off the trail on that single turn out between us. That actually worked. The rider in front of me had no place to go, so I told him to stay put. Examining the hillside above my little string, I realized that it was a cut bank about 15 feet high. The hillside above it might be doable. All four of my mules had 20 or 30 years experience doing the impossible in the high lonesome. Leading Julie and her three ancient friends we scrambled up and teetered balancing on the edge of the cut bank. I motioned the private rider to get by in a hurry, but he thought it would be a good idea to stop and talk. He had a question for me. He said," How in the world do you do something like that?" Thinking of my great old mules, I just said, "It's the difference between being an amateur and a professional." He looked mostly insulted and it wasn't until later that I realized that he thought I was referring to people rather than mules. It pissed him off enough to get him moving and my string of magic mules got down before the cut bank could come down with us. I don't know why he was insulted. I didn't say a word about his fringed buckskins, chromed chop ax, Davy Crocket hat and other "western" paraphernalia sported by him and his friends. As we continued back along the trail, Kid and his riders dropped in behind me and we continued until we reached the open spaces on the bench. When the private party had finished passing us, we returned to the downhill trail and continued downhill to Cascade Valley where we would make out next camp.

If ever I were again to have to ride the same trial twice on the same day, this is the one I would least mind. Cascade Valley is a very special place. You switchback down the steep hillside covered in old pines. When you reach the bottom, you swim across a big, deep creek to a lush meadow in the bottom of the classic glacial canyon. The flat bottom is filled with meadow after meadow. The sheer walls are home to many cascading waterfalls. A truly beautiful place.

That's about all the trail encounters for that particular trip, I seem to remember a few incidents that don't qualify as trail encounters, but what the heck, I remember the older packers playing a practical joke on Kid involving a cantaloupe. It must have been bad because he told them God would send them to hell for it. Most of the odd things involved lots of champagne and drunks. Howard wanted to fire the hiking guide for bad language. One guest got out her samuri sword and chased people with it. When people were taking pictures of packers with the snow and champagne bottles and Cockburn didn't think it was funny enough so he dropped his pants. Hairiest thing I've ever seen until someone nailed him with a snowball. Have you noticed that things get a little more extreme when Craig isn't there to keep us in line. Well actually that may not be true because I think he was somehow involved in the cantaloupe thing.

On another Henkes trip, probably a few years before this one they had a new guest named Kingsley who got into a few problems. This was the first year when people worried about giardia. Most people carried filters. Some of us just drank the creek water or boiled some in camp. It seemed that Kingsly just didn't get it. He just took about two cups of clean water and figured that that would be plenty for an 8-mile hike on a hot day. The packers found him along the trail almost unconscious from dehydration. He was beside a creek but wouldn't drink from it. The packers were each carrying 2 cans of soda. It was kinda a treat for the trip but they gave him all four cans. He never seemed to understand that that was special. After that day some of the other guests took over filtering water for him. I never heard him thank anyone.

Toward the end of the trip we were in Northern Yosemite. We had to turn off the trail we were on to get to our night's camp at Peeler Lake. Either the hiking guide or the head packer had marked the turn off. It was so well marked that it made me laugh. It included a row of big white rocks across the trail, two more rows with arrow points towards the camp, three white paper plates on the tree, writing on them said "Peeler Lake Camp", "Henkes Party Camp", "Hikers turn here". Guess who missed it and went seven miles farther over the pass. Craig took an extra horse that far in the dark to bring him safely back.

Often on long trips like this where the friendships are long term, someone will bring an especially funny joke and it will become the "trip joke" and be told over and over again. Pretty soon it reaches the point where someone says the first few words of the joke and everyone laughs. Well, this trip actually had a "trip joke," It goes," What is the difference between a porcupine and a red Porsche? The answer is that a porcupine has the pricks on the outside and a red Porsche has the prick on the inside." I know it's an old joke but we thought it was hysterical. At the end of the trip they picked us up out of Twin Lakes near Bridgeport. They stuffed us in a couple of vans and hauled us back to Rock Creek Pack There they put all our duffle and camp equipment on the wooden docks. Then each person would hike down to the parking lot, get their car and come up to the docks to load their stuff. In addition, this time was filled with good byes, hugs, addresses and even retellings of the joke. Suddenly everyone froze in unison and stared at the next vehicle in line. It was Kingsly and he was driving a red Porsche. End of story- total hysteria- uncontrollable laughter-the end.

Well, since this was supposed to be a set of tales of meetings on the trail perhaps, I should end with such a meeting. How about many years ago when we worked for Mt Whitney Pack Trains and all of us were young and foolish. Near Little Whitney Meadow on the Kern Plateau we found a sick hiker left alone in a camp. He was way too sick to hike but was sure he could ride. His trail partner had left him several days ago to go for help. But in those days, we had little way of knowing how that had turned out. We were leading a number of empty horses and mules as we had taken in a spot trip. We offered the sick guy to haul him and his stuff out if he would pay our boss for the use of the stock. We pushed hard and I'm pretty sure we made it out in a day. We were all young enough to be real proud of our big rescue. What we missed was the pack string from a different outfit on the way in to rescue our sick guy. They had been hired by our guy's partner to go and bring him. Unfortunately, it all ended in a big dogfight between the pack outfits and we got our butts chewed by our boss for messing with someone else's rescue.

Guess my last trail story should end up below the pack station at Agnew. So, we had left the John Muir Trail near Shadow Lake, dropped down into the canyon and were climbing up a long, steep, sandy hillside to Agnew. The packer ahead of me had a tail mule who was pretty mean and would try to kick anyone he could. That's why he was on the end of the string. After several days on the trail together I had heard the packer warn hikers time and again about moving clear of that end mule. This time however it was the hiker that was the problem. He informed my packer that he had every right to be on that trail and we would have to leave the trail and go around him. After a really long explanation of why that wasn't a good idea, the packer gave up and passed him on the uphill side. The hiker stayed right in the middle of the trail and when the end mule reached him that mule took one long step to the right and drop kicked that guy clear off the trail. Luckily there were no big rocks on that sandy hill. He bounced and rolled about 100 yards to the bottom of the hill. We saw him later at the pack station and he seemed to be okay. Maybe he had changed his mind about who had the right of way on the trail as he didn't say anything more.

SOMETIMES A HERO…

When it's your turn to tell packing tales around the campfire, there is often a hero in your tale. Usually, it is the packer as he is saddled with the chores that include the most danger and require the most strength, skill, and bravery. Sometimes the hero is a horse or mule that is living up to the tradition of equines in fictional stories. The cook is very seldom the hero as there isn't a whole lot of derring-do in the kitchen. The other factor that keeps a cook from telling her own stories is that it looks a lot like bragging, which you really don't want to do. All of that aside, here is a story with no horses or mules, no packers, no trails, and no campfires, but the cook does get to be the hero, or maybe the complete fool as is decided by pure luck.

This series of events took place at the Rock Creek Pack Station. It was during late August and almost every hand working for the outfit and every animal were out in the backcountry working on a trip. I was in the supply room back of the kitchen pulling supplies for my next trip. I had come in off a trip the night before and had one day to prepare for my next trip which would hit the trail the next morning. Most of the corrals were empty and the only other person on the place was Herb London, the boss. At this point Herb was in his eighties and pretty crippled up. He was in the station office struggling with the paperwork.

My quiet pursuit of getting all my food ready was suddenly interrupted when a young girl ran in the kitchen door. She was about eight to ten years old and seemed to be in quite a hurry. She asked to use our phone. I started to explain to her that the boss didn't let us loan out the phone but that there was a pay phone about 100 yards down the road. She started to cry and babbled something about an emergency. I figured she needed some real help. I patted her on the shoulder and said, "Show me." She led me out the kitchen door and pointed down the station driveway to where it crossed Rock Creek Road. On the other side of the road there was a car. It looked like it had backed down the drive and gone straight across the road and off the other side. That other side is a steep jumble of boulders and aspens leading hundreds of feet down to the lake. The only thing holding the car from going off was that the two front tires had stopped against the asphalt berm on the far side. The rest of the car was balanced on the jumble of aspen branches. There didn't seem to be anything else holding it up, and it was bouncing gently in the wind.

Hurrying down the drive, I could hear that the engine was still running on the car. There were two young men with panicked looks on their faces staring helplessly at the car. Later I would learn that they had left the car parked next to the office while they arranged a horseback ride for their little sister. They left it running and the automatic in second gear. I guess it became a tug of war between the steep drive and the forward gear which ended in the car slowly easing down the hill, across the road, and out into space, only to be stopped at the last moment by the five-inch berm against the front tires.

My first thought was that it was way too late to call for help as the nearest tow truck was at least twenty-five miles away. There was no one else around to help and I sure wasn't gonna get Herb hurt by involving him in this. I told the kids to stay away from the car while I got my truck. Living in the Owens Valley I, of course, drove a 4-wheel drive pick-up and carried a tow chain. I backed the truck down the hill to the front of the car. I hooked the chain to my trailer hitch and one of the boys hooked it under the front of the car. I put the truck in 4-wheel low and locked in the hubs. One of the boys had reached in the car window and shifted the gears on the car from second to park before I got there. So now I told him to reach in and pop it into neutral then jump clear. He said that he was going to jump in and steer the car while I towed it. I'm sure I did serious damage to his male pride, because I told him if he tried to get in the car I would unhook my truck and leave them there. I know that was mean but I kept seeing mental images of the car crashing down the hill with him in it. Anyway, he backed off. I got in the truck and took up the slack. He popped the thing into neutral and jumped clear. I accelerated the truck and pulled that car out of its cradle of branches and back onto the road. Then I just sat there and shook as I realized that I hadn't really known if that truck would pull that big car out of the rocks and aspens. "Stupid bitch" was all I could think to myself.

So, we unhitched the car and the kids left. They thanked me, waved, and drove off. I put the truck away and went back to outfitting my next trip. Another day, another dollar. I might have been a hero for a few seconds, but I could just as easily have been the fool. Guess it mostly depends on luck.

BLIZZARD ON MONO PASS

Not long ago I was tellin' some stories about love in the High Sierras, and I got a little sidetracked talking about the troubles that happen when you have to work with a couple that is trying to cope with the fact that their trails were startin' to split up. When such a pair are partnered-up on the job, it can often interfere with getting their work done right. Cat and Tom were to the spittin' and clawin' stage of their break-up when they were putting together a trip for me.

I was base camped in Pioneer Basin with Spike, a white-haired gentleman from Arizona who was packing part-time that summer. Tom and Cat were assigned to bring us a new set of guests, all their equipment and a four-day resupply for the kitchen. Seems like they got in an argument about who was supposed to gather and pack what. Anyhow it ended up that they forgot the tents. Our guests were two couples so we only needed two tents. The first night was clear and not too cold so our guests decided that they were perfectly happy sleepin' out under the stars.

By the next morning, the situation had deteriorated just a tad. It was so cloudy that you couldn't see any part of the sky. You also couldn't see the top third of any of the pine trees surrounding our camp. What you could see were the first few snowflakes whipping by in the cold driving wind. First, we put up the kitchen tarp and moved all our gear in under it. We stuffed the guests' duffle and bedrolls under the tables. It made an adequate shelter for sittin' under during the day, but there was no way in God's green earth that the six of us were going to be able to spend a stormy night under it.

Being pretty good at procrastinating, I decided to wait until 9:00 in the morning to see if there was any break in the weather. If it still looked bad at that point, I planned to ride out after the tents. I couldn't wait any later than that as a round trip ride from Pioneer Basin over Mono Pass to the pack station and back was about a nine-hour ride, even in good weather. Later one of the other station packers would ask me why I didn't send Spike instead of my going which probably bruised his pride. Well, I had years more experience on Mono Pass than he did and I had the world's best riding mule. And sometimes a gals gotta do what a gals gotta do.

The morning wore on and the weather got worse, so it was time to hit the trail. I layered on all the clothes I could without looking like my nephew in his snowsuit, and Abby mule and I set out. As we left Pioneer Basin, the trail dropped downhill into Mono Canyon and the weather slacked off a bit. Then we started our climb toward the summit of Mono Pass which is just barely below 12,000 feet. As the wind and snow got wilder, I put on extra gloves and tied my wild rag over the top of my hat to keep it on my head and to fold the sides down over my ears. Looked stupid but beat all heck out of freezing to death.

By the time we got above Trail Lake, we were in a flat out blizzard. We were headin' straight into the wind and the most I could see ahead was a vague outline of Abby's ears. By the time we reached the flat up by Summit Lake, I had no real idea of where we were. Finally, I just tied my reins around the saddle horn and trusted Abby to find our way. It was real amazing. She would turn her face directly into the wind and point her ears straight ahead as if that would help her find her way. Then she would walk four or five steps and stop. Her ears would be packed full of snow and she would drop her head and shake the snow out. Then she would face forward again and start all over. At one point we were winding our way through some huge grey shapes that I figured must be giant boulders. Suddenly Abby stopped and dropped her head down to examine some things that were moving at the base of the boulders. As she and I both realized that the shapes were backpackers taking shelter from the storm, Abby raised her head and taking tiny, careful steps worked her way around the hikers without stepping on anyone.

She continued on into the teeth of the storm for what was probably an hour until we topped over the summit of the pass. As we dropped down the far side of the pass the wind and snow started to slack off. Gradually my vision cleared enough that I could see that Abby and I were smack-dab on the trail, right where we wanted to be. I've ridden some great animals in my life, but right at that moment I had to figure that Abby was the best of them.

As we worked our way down the Sandy Switchbacks above Ruby Lake, we started to run out of falling snow and howling wind. We were still wading through snow and the temp was colder 'n snake snot, but it was sure as shootin' nicer than it had been on the top of the pass. Suddenly it looked like we might not die up here after all. As the relief of this realization cut through me, I relaxed enough to also realize that I needed to pee. What can I say? That's how it was. There were no other people anywhere around so we rode off the trail into the hidden shelter of some trees. Getting off I started to struggle with all my layers of clothes. Sometimes being a girl is a real pain. Holding Abby by her reins, I hunkered down in the snow to take care of the situation. At that point, Abby gave me a funny look, sidled over next to me, squatted and joined me in peeing in the snow. I don't know what kind of bonding that was, but mostly I was glad she wasn't uphill from me.

The next couple of hours to the pack station were not too bad except for the biting cold. By the time we got there I was so cold that I knew if I got off, I might not be able to get back on. Fortunately, Phil and Jamie, the two nicest people in the mountains, were in the yard when I arrived. After a brief explanation, Abby and I waited while Jamie brought me a steaming cup of coffee and Phil prepared the tents. Within ten minutes, we were headed back up the trail with two tents hanging from my saddle horn.

Heading back over the pass was way easier as the storm broke up around us and started to move off to the east. There was still snow to wade through and cold to deal with, but the falling snow and miserable wind gradually stopped. Now that I had safely acquired the tents, the next thing I had to worry about was getting back to camp in time to cook dinner. At Rock Creek, dinner time is regularly at 6:00. Of course, appetizers were supposed to be up by 5:00 which pretty much meant I needed to start cooking by around 4 PM. To make it by that time, I would have had to cut at least two hours off the regular time for such a ride. Abby had already put in a really tough day so there was no way I was going to push her. The unspoken rule at that kind of altitude was that you never pushed your animal faster than a walk.

Once we topped the pass, Abby's walk started to pick up speed. Maybe she felt good heading back to camp. Maybe she was lonesome for the other horses and mules. Lookin' to entertain myself on the way back, I was wondering if we could finish this trip in some kind of record time, silly thoughts but it helps keep you from fallin' asleep in the saddle.

To my honest surprise we pulled into camp at 4:10 PM. We had round tripped the pass in 7 hours and 10 minutes. Even better, Spike had built a windbreak around the kitchen and already started dinner. Spike allowed as how he didn't much care for cooking and offered to unsaddle and rub down my poor tired mule if I would take over the cooking.

After a dinner of BBQ chicken and with our guests all tucked away in their nice snug tents, Spike and I sat by the campfire and talked. We both allowed as how the day had ended a whole lot better than it started.

MOUNTAIN DOGS

Many pack outfits in the High Sierra don't allow their packers to bring dogs with them when they work. The problems in bringing your dog along are legion. First off, they aren't allowed in the National Parks where a good half of our trips travel. If you have a good dog, he might help you gather stock, or chase bears out of camp, or be a big hit with the guests. If he's not such a good dog, he will probably chase and kill wildlife, spook the horses on the trail, attack other dogs or people on the trail, steal food out of the kitchen, or get lost in the wilderness.

One of my big surprises when I went to work for Rock Creek Pack Station was that I was the only one there who hadn't brought my dog. The Londons who run the outfit love dogs and usually bring their own to the station. Herb London likes to tell stories of all the times in his long and colorful career that his life has been saved by having a good dog along. Seems like everyone who owns a dog brings him along when he works for the RC.

Phil and Jamie, who have been with Rock Creek for close to forty years, used to have a great little border collie named Teddy. He was the cutest, funniest little guy and all the guests adored him. Eventually he passed away from old age. Phil and Jamie were really sad but didn't get another dog. Several years later their in-laws in Arizona raised three litters of Aussie x border collie pups so they could push Phil and Jamie into getting a new dog. Phil and Jamie finally ended up with two puppies, one from each of the first two litters. Most of the puppies from all three litters ended up belonging to packer folks in the Eastern Sierra. Everyone calls them Phil-and-Jamie-dogs. I even ended up with one of them, though my dog, Red Man, is the only goofy one. Figures.

Jim and Kelly Brumfield, another long-time packer couple, had a golden retriever named Kegger. He was quiet and sweet. When he was still young enough to travel in the mountains, he would somehow manage to persuade the guests that they should give him one of the chairs around the campfire for his own. I would come by and find him just sitting there in a chair by the fire like he thought he was a paying guest.

When Tim, the world's best-looking packer, first came to work at Rock Creek, he brought a pair of Queensland healers. Ralph and CJ were litter brothers, but they fought all the time. One time I was on a base camp at Evans Camp on Mono Creek with Jason and Maggie. Jason, a barrel-chested Basque from Canada, was our head packer. Maggie, a cute little Samoan girl, was wrangling this trip. Tim and his dogs were at Bench Camp, a few miles up canyon. It's kinda a complicated story, but it all started out with some Boy Scouts coming to Tim's camp for help. It seemed like one teenaged scout was real sick. After waiting a couple of days for him to get better, the rest of the troop had moved on leaving the sick boy with an assistant leader and his younger son. The leader came to Tim's camp looking for help. Tim rode down to our camp to get Jason who was an EMT. Jason thought it was most likely altitude sickness and talked the leader into helping the boy to move down canyon to our camp since it was at a lower elevation.

Two of my guests were doctors and consulted with Jason on the boy's condition. He was actually in pretty poor shape. He definitely couldn't make it out over a 12,000-foot pass. Tim was leading out a string of empty mules the next morning so he agreed to move early and fast so he could send back a helicopter for the kid. Since he wouldn't have time to worry about his dogs on the trail, he dropped the heelers off at our camp. To keep them from following him, he tied them to a saddle by the picket line.

Later that morning Maggie went to saddle up the horses for a day ride. She found that Tim's dogs were tied to her saddle. When she tried to move them so she could use her saddle, they went after each other. The yipping, barking, and snarling led us all to the picket line for a major dog fight. By the time we had them separated, Ralph was spurting bright arterial blood from his right foreleg. Jason grabbed him and stuck a finger in the hole in his leg. We shared horrified looks as we realized that Ralph had a severed artery and would bleed to death if Jason moved his hand.

In the packing business we always take what we have and do the best that we can. Luckily, we had doctors and an EMT. I scrubbed down the kitchen table cloth with lots of bleach. Jason found suture needles and thread in the vet supplies for the horses. One fisherman had several hemostats. The horse kit also included some anesthetic. The doctors didn't have a surgical kit, but they did have expertise and some Lidocain. Everyone scrubbed up as best they could. It looked like a scene from MASH with guests and crew alike pitching in to hold Ralph's legs, body and head still. I got to hold the flashlight pointed at the hole in his leg. Discovering that CJ's tooth had punctured rather than severed the artery, the doctors managed to repair Ralph enough to save his life. His bandages were vet wrap and duct tape. The cone around his neck to keep him from chewing on his bandages was made out of cardboard box. He was put to bed in my sleeping bag.

That afternoon our group finally got to go on the day ride that had been sidetracked by the dog fight. I stayed in camp to watch over Ralph and to wait for the helicopter that we hoped would come for the sick boy. Around 2 o'clock the chopper showed up and air lifted the scout to the Fresno Hospital. The paramedic who examined him said that he only had about another 24 hours left before his altitude sickness would have become fatal. Ralph slept through the whole thing. What a day!! When Tim returned the next day, he told us about the wreck he and his mules had had trying to hurry out over Mono Pass. He was pretty amazed at how his dog looked, but real happy when he figured out how everyone had pitched in to save Ralph's life.

Several years later Ralph played an interesting role in another High Sierra dog story. Tari Justice, a nurse from the Reno area, was one of the really great backcountry cooks. Probably still is, just not full-time. She was even on the Rock Creek team that won World Champion Pack Team at Mule Days. Just to keep her hand in, she works several weeks each summer. In the past on these trips she usually brought her dog Jessica.

Jessica was a sweet, smart little border collie. She was Tari's full-time partner and best friend.

One summer as Tim and I were putting together a trip from Rock Creek to Mammoth, the outfitter came up to me in the kitchen and handed me a letter and a small wooden box. The letter was one of the saddest I had ever seen. It was from Tari and explained that Jessica had died suddenly. It was obvious that Tari was heartbroken. She said she couldn't bring herself to go to the mountains that summer. All she asked was that the next crew members going to Silver Pass Meadow would scatter Jessica's ashes there for her. Tim and I were headed there so we got the little wooden box with Jessica's ashes.

Our second night's camp was at Silver Pass Meadow. So, after dinner, I took the box and headed out away from camp. Tim said he would go, too, and it seemed natural that his dogs, CJ and Ralph, should join little Jessica's funeral. It was a beautiful spot, a small green meadow ankle-deep in wildflowers. Granite cliffs rose above us catching the golden rays of the late sun. A hundred yards away, the mules and horses grazed peacefully along the stream. Packer folk not being real big on serious words, we didn't say anything, just scattered the ashes among the wildflowers. I stood there and thought about Jessica running in the meadow, and I stared away at the peaks so Tim couldn't see that I was crying.

Just then Patty, an old club-footed black mule, looked up from her grazing and noticed we were pouring the ashes into the grass. Assuming that it was most likely grain, she headed our way at a high trot. Arriving at our location, she buried her nose in the grass and started snuffling around looking for goodies. She inhaled some of the ashes and snorted them out her nose. Ralph, being born a herding dog, decided it was his job to chase the mule off. He heeled her and she kicked at him with both hind feet. He jumped up and grabbed hold of her tail. She spun clear around with Ralph swinging out from the end of her tail. When that didn't rid her of the persistent dog, she swatted her tail forward between her hind legs. Ralph came loose and popped out, rolling between her front legs. Surprised by the dog under her nose, Patty took off across the meadow at a run. Ralph took off after her. Pretty soon all the horses, mules, and dogs were running, barking, snorting, and bucking around the meadow. I couldn't help myself. I just sat down in the grass and laughed and laughed. I kinda hoped Jessica's spirit was out there running with them.

After our return to the pack station at the end of the trip, I wrote Tari a letter about Jessica's send-off. I wasn't real sure how she would take it. Eventually I got a note back from Tari. All it said was, "Thanks. Jessica would have loved it."

ONCE UPON A MAGIC PLACE

Telling tales around the campfire there are a few things you might want to leave out, like maybe personal stuff such as romances or the feeling of riding all day with a sore on your butt, but what I'm talking about right now are those hidden places in the High Sierra that are so special that you can't bring yourself to share them with even your best friends. Now, you and I both know that the most average day in the high lonesome can still be spectacular enough to live in your memory forever. And even a long, dry day dragging a reluctant string down a dusty, old hillside can be enough to make you want to sing out loud. Above and beyond these times are a few places that are so special that you just can't quite bring yourself to talk about them. But now that I am gettin' old enough that I may never see most of them again, I thought I might share some of them with you guys. In the back of my head I think of them as "magic places."

Starting out with Strawberry Meadow, it's not really a secret, just a place that people sorta forgot about. It's near Crabtree Meadows, one of the best known places in the Sierra. Crabtree is where the PCT joins the John Muir Trail. It's where the southern end of the JMT turns to take you to the highest spot in the 48 states, Mount Whitney. Everybody knows where it is and almost everybody has been there. What most people don't know is that the trail used to cross this area just about a half-mile downstream at Strawberry Meadow. To get there you can find a piece of the old trail or you can climb down the little water falls below the camp at the lower edge of Lower Crabtree Meadow. Arriving at Strawberry it becomes immediately obvious that this was once an important camp site. There is a small fenced meadow for grazing and a campsite with tables and a bear box along the creek. Long ago this was a serious camp, but more recently the park must have had a trail crew living here for a while. Now that you have found the camp you need to get across the creek. The water is too wide and too deep to wade across. I have crossed it on mule back and there is a down tree you can crawl across if you don't happen to have a mule. Once across the water, head down stream for maybe a hundred yards. There is a little bench twenty feet back from the water covered in grass that is almost painfully green and tangled in masses of blooming wildflowers. Partially covered by the foliage is a hot spring, fifteen feet wide and about a foot and a half deep. It's nice and warm, maybe ninety degrees and you can just lay there soaking among the wildflowers. You won't even need a swimsuit as the dozens of hikers passing by less than half a mile away have absolutely no idea that Strawberry is there.

Sometimes the simplest things can prove to be magic if you just take the time to look at them. Near the southern edge of Sequoia National Park, the PCT crosses an area called Guyot between Crabtree and Rock Creek. Actually, it must have been named for some bigwig in the Park Service because you go up Guyot mountain, summit Guyot Pass, then cross Guyot Flats all on the PCT. The area around Guyot Flats had been burned over seventy or eighty years before. Right next to the trail in the middle of the flats was a tall, burned stump. Never paid it no mind except that the trail bent around it. Then one day we had to wait at that exact spot for the rest of our party to catch up to us. We got pretty bored waiting and started wondering about the stump. First we decided that it was a foxtail pine from the tiny tree rings it had. Foxtails are close relatives of the famous Bristlecones. Like them it is a high altitude, desert edge tree. Because of the lack of moisture, they are extremely slow growing with very narrow growth rings. Then we decided that it was burned in the same fire as the rest of the down trees in the area, but the shape of the break indicated that it was probably broken off some time before the fire. One of the guests had a pretty powerful magnifying glass, so we set out to count its rings. So, our final results told us that the foxtail pine on Guyot Flat had blown down more than eighty years ago, then was burned over in the fire, and had lived for more than 700 years before it fell.

Another place easily missed but filled with touches of magic is in the Pizona near the Nevada border where we follow the wild horses. Of course, the horses themselves are pretty awe-inspiring; newborn foals, fighting stallions, pregnant mares, bachelor bands of young studs. But that is what we all hope and expect to see. Less expected are things like an ephemeral lake that is there in the spring and gone in the summer. There is a pass where we would stop for lunch in the pinon trees. Closer looks found evidence that this had once been an early Indian camp. The basaltic rocks were carved with ancient petroglyphs. On the ridge above the campsite were areas where you could find piles of obsidian flakes where people had sat and flaked arrowheads. Just below the campsite were flat rocks with grinding holes where they had ground the pine nuts into flour. There were also circles of rocks called house rings left where they had held down the bottom edges of brush shelters. The Paiutes lived in this high, cold area in the winter because that was when they could harvest the pine nuts.

In other areas in among the sage brush and pinon trees, there were startling things to find like a desert apricot, a wild relative to some of our fruit trees that is a big, long bush about twenty feet long and five feet high completely covered in pink blossoms like those on a peach tree. There is also big sage, called that because the bushes are ten or fifteen feet tall. Living and hiding in the big sage are tiny little dark brown rabbits. I think they are called pygmy rabbits. In the willow near rare springs there are also miner's cats which look like a taupe cat with a tail that is longer than its body and is black-and-white striped like a raccoon tail.

There are numerous petroglyph sites hidden in the brush. The pictures on them usually include sheep, some other animals, abstract people, weapons, and always outlines of human hands. I actually found one site that had feet instead of hands. Having seen petroglyph and pictograph sites all over the eastern Sierra and the Great Basin, this rare site was the only one I ever saw that had feet.

Right next to the old dirt road that led from our camp to the Upper Pizona spring there is a strange but obviously volcanic outcropping. Finally figured out that it was a lahar. That's where a volcanic vent pushes lava to the surface right in the middle of a lake or maybe a glacier. The water boils and melts any snow, mixes with rock, hot lava, dirt, steam, and anything else available. Then it all flows downhill until it cools enough to harden in place.

Leaving the magic of the Pizona, let us now return to some of the magic things in the Sierra. Along the JMT, up canyon from The Devil's Postpile, you will find three lakes named for the daughters of John Muir. Lake Gladys is a fair-sized lake sandwiched between the trail and the cliff edge above the river canyon. There are several campsites there, a swimmable lake and terrific views of the canyon. The winds can be fierce and if you don't weigh down your tent with rocks, it might take flight over the canyon. Also, the lake water is pretty darn cold. In fact, sometimes all the water in the whole Sierra seems pretty darn cold. Sometimes I feel that I would trade my soul for a chance at a warm bath. With that in mind, I remember when an old friend and hiking guide named Ollie told me that the next time I camped at Gladys, I should take a little stroll over the glaciated knob just north of the campsite. What I found was a land locked tarn, a small pond fifteen feet across and a couple of feet deep. It had no inlet or outlet. It filled in the winter then just sat there all summer soaking up sun. The water was clean unless you stirred up the mud on the bottom. Nothing organic in it except for a few caddis flies in their little camouflage suits. A nice, warm pool just waiting for someone like me. Yeah…

Well, now I find myself thinking of so many memorable spots that I don't know which to talk about. How about Silver Pass Meadow where you climb your horse through a stair-step waterfall up a sheer cliff to reach a lovely little meadow pocketed among granite cliffs? There you will find wildflowers, good graze, sweet campsites, sunset views over all the Sierra to the south, and even trees with 150-year-old pictures carved by the Basque sheepherders back in the 1800's. What about Peter Pande Lake? High in a hanging valley above Grassy Lake, the outlet from this fair-sized lake cuts a narrow gash through the smooth, glaciated rocks. The faster the water moves, the narrower and deeper that slot grows until it blows to the surface in a natural Jacuzzi big enough for a dozen people. Just a few feet away the water leaving that bubbling pool leaps off a cliff to become a 100-foot-high waterfall.

You know when I started this story, I made a list of really special places I wanted to talk about. Now on the list I found a note that said Upper Rush Creek and I couldn't for the life of me remember what made me list it. It's a rocky piece of trail between a reservoir called Waugh Lake and Donohue Pass on the south boundary of the park. Nice enough country but nothing earth-shaking. After some serious thinking I came up with a memory of one time when Matt Taylor and I had to camp just above the crossing there because some other packer had beaten us to the camp we usually used. I do remember the layover day there when Matt was going to wrangle bareback. He was just young enough and new enough that he felt he had to show off a little. So he swung up on the bareback horse, missed, went on over and landed on his back on the ground on the other side. He wasn't real pleased by how humorous I found it. But dang, I'd been in this business more than thirty years and never actually seen anyone do that. Well, not except in cartoons anyway. But that story wasn't why I put that place on the list. Later that same day, the packers and guests had all ridden up to Marie Lakes. I got to stay behind and babysit the camp. Usually it didn't bother me, but in that case, I was feeling grouchy and put upon. I was stamping around camp feeling sorry for myself. Then something caught my eye and I realized that nature had dropped a tiny piece of magic right there just for me. It was just like a precious little photo. It was smooth rock polished by glaciers and flowing water. There was a little pothole filled with water from last night's storm. It was right at the base of an ancient, twisted pine. Beyond the pine and silhouetted against the sky was the rim of Island Pass with a single sharp peak behind it. The water in the hole was perfectly still and reflected an unbroken picture of the pine, the pass, the peak and the blue, blue sky. The edge of the pothole was framed all the way around in blooming white heather. It was tiny and it was perfect and I held my breath staring at it.

Then there was the place I have always thought of as "the" magic place. We were on one of the many Henkes trips. There were too many hikers for a single trip so we were running two parallel trips. We came out of Kennedy Meadows in northern Yosemite. Whenever we made camp a park ranger would show up to tell us we needed to be farther apart. It was one of those trips where lots of things went wrong and you kinda wished you had stayed home. One of my mules tipped herself over backwards on a log and by the time we got things straight I had a broken thumb for a souvenir. At one point we camped in a really ugly spot. In retrospect I think it was in an old avalanche path. The hillside was barren except for scraggly little trees all about four feet tall and crooked. The hills above our site were mostly rocks and brush. Sounds pretty exciting already, doesn't it. I can't begin to tell you where we were, just that we were below Bond Pass and Dorothy Lake. The next day was a layover day which would normally have been great, but this place was so ugly I really didn't want to stay.

The next day after breakfast was finished and camp cleaned up, I was lookin' for a place to get in a creek, or haul water away from the creek so I could bathe and wash my hair. Somebody told me that there was a good-sized pool up creek from our camp. I grabbed up a bucket and a towel. I was hoping the pool was out of sight of the camp as this kind of activity doesn't usually involve clothes for me. Well. I found the pool alright. It was big, round, and deep. Bad thing was that it was actually right between the guests' tents, still right in camp. Interesting thing was that there was no creek above that point, the water was coming directly out of a big hole in the ground. Looked like privacy might be a problem so I decided I would hike further up canyon in hopes of finding another creek. The canyon floor was dry and sandy with no sign of there ever having been water there. I went about one quarter mile with the dry canyon floor slowly turning into volcanic basalt. Then I came around a corner and found the stream again. It was flowing down the canyon and disappeared into a hole.

As I continued up canyon along the creek, it was like walking on the yellow brick road or some other enchanted trail. The bottom and walls of the canyon gradually changed from dirty grey sand and blackish boulders into white volcanic tuft. And the white stones soon came to be sculpted by the flowing water. Eventually I was walking in a waist high garden of white abstract carvings and tall, blooming penstemon, tiger lilies, columbine, and fireweed. Ahead I could see where a white ridge of stone blocked the canyon and there was a large white cave where the stream entered the valley. I couldn't picture anything prettier than this so I took a bucket of water and went off the trail to a private spot in the rocks to bathe and wash my hair. Later, all clean and dressed, I sat among the flowers and stones along the creek letting my hair dry in the sun. It seemed so magic that I was thinking that this fairy tale really needed a handsome prince. While I was laughing to myself about that, I heard a noise and looked up to see a handsome young man making his way down the other side of the creek. He was not a prince, but a guest on my trip. Aside from that he pretty much met the description. He stood close to the creek and mouthed the words, "This is a magic place." I smiled and nodded. Then I gestured downstream and indicated that there was more to come. He pointed upstream past the place where the stream came out of the white cave and said, "There's more. Don't stop until you get to the cascade." Then we went our separate ways.

I left the bucket by the stream and followed a faint trail up the white rock ridge past the cave mouth. The dry canyon stretched on before me. The stream was back underground. As I hiked on I left the area with the white rocks and was back on sand over jumbled basalt. It seemed that over the years the canyon had been repeatedly buried under various lava flows. In many spots the lava had buried the stream bed. While hiking on this section, I could actually hear the stream flowing through the rocks piled as much as thirty feet beneath where I was walking.

Eventually I reached the place where the stream was back on the surface and you could watch it disappear where it hit a black rock wall and plunged into a deep green pool and vanished underground. Continuing up the stream from there I eventually rounded a corner and found the cascade. At this point there was another lava flow that had blocked the stream. Instead of going under this flow the stream was going over it. It was high, very wide and had even stair-steps of rock. It looked sorta like a flood flowing down the Capitol steps. Like everything else in this canyon, it was amazing.

Realizing that my little hike had used up most of the afternoon, I headed home to fix dinner. I passed all these amazing sites again and remembered to pick up my bucket. As the guests drifted through cocktail hour, dinner, and time around the campfire, I was puzzled to realize that no one had mentioned the stream. Maybe no one had gone there. Maybe no one believed those of us who had. Eventually I ran into Tom, the guy I met on the stream. I asked him if he had shared it with anyone else. It turned out that he hadn't. We ended up agreeing that we didn't want to dim the magic by talking about it. So we never did.

It wasn't until this summer, about twenty years later, that I actually shared this place. You see I got an email from Gail Hobson, a long-time hiking friend. And the email said that she had just finished a trip into northern Yosemite and would I believe that just above her camp she had discovered a place in a dry canyon where a whole stream came right up out of the ground. So I finally told someone about the magic place.

THE LONG, LONG TRIP

When fans of the High Sierra get together for a little bragging session, it usually turns into claims of having completed certain trails like the Pacific Crest or the John Muir. As you probably know the PCT reaches along the crest of the mountains from the California-Mexico Border to the Washington-Canada border. The Muir reaches from Yosemite Valley to the top of Mount Whitney along the "Range of Light." Those two trails actually overlap for most of 200 miles. When you plan your own trip and travel it alone, you can usually cover the Muir in three weeks or less. However, when you work for pack outfits, you get to go where they send you and the chance to pick your own route almost never happens. In fact, I first set foot on the southern end on the John Muir Trail when I went to work for Mount Whitney Pack Trains in 1964. Thirty-some years later in the year 2000, I was still not finished. There was still one three-mile piece of trail between Tyndal Creek and Big Horn Plateau that I hadn't traveled. It wasn't anything special, but I just never got there. Dozens of times I just missed it. We would come in over Shepherd Pass and then head north, or start south of Whitney, travel up to Wright Creek and then cut down to the Kern, or even come up the Kern then cut up to Wallace and then head south. In 2001, working for Rock Creek, I finally got chosen to work the Longest Trip and finally completed the Muir. Actually, that was one of the less exciting things about that trip. Lotta stuff happened on those twenty-four days.

First off, I was getting way too old for this kind of job. I remember being forty-four when Craig refused to hire me for Rock Creek being as how that made me an "old" pack cook that no outfit would want, being as they were reputed to be dirty and mean. At the time of this trip I was fifty-seven and really starting to feel it. Hoping to keep my job as long as possible, I was the only employee that never asked for special treatment like, for instance getting to go on the long trip. I knew that Craig was cutting me some slack already such as having the guys lift my saddle for me when I was saddling up and carry my cooking water up from the stream to the kitchen It was kinda embarrassing for me but it let me keep going. Time would prove that I was only a couple of years away from two major back surgeries, so I guess I really needed the help. Hearing about the plans for the long trip made my mouth water, but I never asked for it and was quietly grateful for the trips I did get. That is, if you can picture me being quiet about anything.

Instead I figured that what I really wanted was the Mammoth Shuttle. That was what the crew called a set of three Mammoth trips back to back. More specifically that meant one seven day trip from Rock Creek to Mammoth. You would end the first trip on a Saturday afternoon and scrambling like a madwoman, clean up everything from that trip, get everything packed for the next trip, and be back on the trail by Sunday morning. That second seven-day trip was the same and ended with a one-night turn-around before the third identical seven-day trip. Getting to do my favorite trip three times in a row sounded real fine to me. Besides it would make a pretty good brag for sitting by the fireplace the next winter.

So, Dr. London gave me the first such trip. When we returned, I braced him and told him I wanted all three. He looked at me kinda slantwise and allowed as how it would probably be too much for me. I guess I looked kinda down about that because Craig told me that I could take the second trip and if I was in really good shape after that, he might let me have the third.

So, the second trip… What can I say? It was made up of about ten of the nicest, funniest people I ever met. The first night we were at Windy Point on Mono Creek and we all stayed up all night. We dragged our beds out on the big smooth rocks and broke out an unreasonable number of bottles of wine. We lay out there all night, drinking wine, telling stories and watching the Perseid Meteor Shower, and, of course, laughing.

The entire trip was like that, laughing all the way. Heck, we even laughed when one lady's horse grabbed a snack alongside the trail in Pocket Meadow. He jerked the clump of grass out by the roots and the roots pulled an entire ground wasp nest out of the ground. We were instantly swarmed by angry, stinging wasps. Every one of us whipped our animals into a run as we raced to beat the wasps to the stream crossing. On the far side of the crossing we seemed to have lost our angry friends and stopped.to assess our damage. As we sat there looking at each other's red welts and hard-breathing animals, we all started laughing again. At the end of the trip Rock Creek picked us up in a van to haul us back from Cold Water to Rock Creek. We even laughed all the way back in the van and when we reached the station, I know I was laughing so hard that I fell out the door of the van. We giggled our way through unpacking and fond farewells. Then I headed for the office to brace Craig about getting the third trip. I felt so damn good that I couldn't imagine his turning me down.

So, I swaggered in and plunked down in a chair with a big shit-eatin' grin on my face and announced I was ready for the third Mammoth run. Craig glanced up and told me I wasn't taking it. As with any other time when a decision went against me, I puffed up and started to argue. He just said that he was sending me home a few days to rest and get caught up, then I was taking out the Long Trip. First thing I did was look around to see who he was talking to, 'cause I knew it couldn't be me. But there was no one else there in the office and indeed, he was giving me the trip.

So, Craig offered me the trip and he said I could have my choice. The trip was changing packers and some guests at the time of the 14th day resupply above Taboose Pass. I was welcome to take either half or the whole thing if I thought I could do it. The only check on that deal was that while I was home, I had to ask my husband, LeRoy, what he thought about my taking all or part of the trip. I was thinking really hard about asking for the first half and worrying about whether I was tough enough for the whole thing. LeRoy is a real smart and sensible guy. Right in the middle of listening to me argue with myself, he stopped me and said that he knew that if I didn't take the whole thing, I would spend the rest of my life regretting it. As usual, he was right. So, I called Craig and told him I wanted the whole trip.

Once I decided to go, getting the whole thing ready in time was "Katie Bar the Door." I had to pack enough clothes for about a week and be prepared to wash them all on the only three layover days on the trip. I also had to create a 24-day menu. The plan had to include meals that would fit on all those moving days, very few slow cooking stews or roasts. I could use the outfit's standardized menu for the first week, but the other seventeen days required a new menu. I would get two resupplies of fresh food on the 7th day and the 14th day. With the exception of the steak dinner, I could not repeat any meals. It took a full day to plan the menu, write the supply lists, and then split it up into the stuff to be ready to go to Tuolumne for the trip start, the stuff to be bought later and packed over Mono Pass to Quail Meadow at the end of the first week, and the final ten-day supply to come in over Taboose Pass with the second packer on the 14th day of the trip. Actually, after I got all that done and got on the trail, it was pretty easy because some other poor soul at the pack station had to clean up my stuff as it came out, shop for each new set and pack it to come in.

Well, truth be told, after fifty-some years of this stuff some of these events start to run together. So, I will just tell this as best I can and leave out the parts that weren't real memorable or maybe some of the embarrassing parts.

So, we started the trip from Tuolumne. It was a small trip with myself cooking, Little Phil Leonti packing and five guests on horseback. Our guests included one old guy named Dave Young who had an injured leg and would have to stay on horseback even when the trail was so rough that everyone else would choose to walk. Of course, he was the only guest who was doing the whole twenty-four days. Seems to me that I later learned that he was raising donkeys and mules down in the Caliente area near Tehachapi. I thought about breeding one of my mares to his jack, but the road was so rough that I couldn't picture hauling a mare with foal by side up there without killing them both. Also, on the trip we had an English woman named Pauline Dodds who had done trips with Rock Creek for years. In fact, she spent her winters in the UK hand-knitting beautiful fishermen's sweaters which she sold for enough money to come to the Sierras for a pack trip each summer. She had been doing that for years and had announced that this would be her last trip as she was getting too old for this stuff. For backup she brought her son James, a newly retired naval sea captain. Our fourth guest was Lyn, another guest who brought a huge scrapbook so we all could share every bit of her family life while we were on the trail. Our final guest for this part of the trip was named Diane. She was a frequent guest with Rock Creek and I had spent a number of trips in her company. I am a big talker but Diane was world class. A few years before this on a wild horse trip in the Pizona, the leader, Tom, told her that there would be NO talking while stalking the mustangs. He taught the guests a set of hand signals which they could use to communicate without spooking the wild horses. In the six or seven hours each day when we could not speak, Diane would just gradually puff up as if she would actually explode if she couldn't talk soon.

Our first day was pretty nice riding up the Lyle Fork of the Tuolumne River to the foot of Donahue Pass. Lots of bears at that camp but no real problems. The next day we crossed Donahue and the Yosemite Park boundary to a camp along Rush Creek. We then followed the John Muir trail over Island Pass, and around Thousand Island Lake below Banner and Ritter. While camped near the head of Thousand Island Lake, I noticed that James had decided that Little Phil had too much work for one packer. First James was hauling wood, holding mules for shoeing, and helping to saddle. As we continued south, it seemed like every day James was learning more packing skills. By the time we camped at Lake Gladys back of Mammoth he was learning to tie a box hitch. Over the next few days, we passed Agnew, the Devils Post Pile, Reds Meadow, Duk Lake, Purple Lake, and ended up at Tully Hole. On that day my mule, Abigail, coliced and I had to lead her the last mile or so to camp. Then I doctored on her a bit and turned her out. Fortunately, the next day was a layover day and I hoped she would have time enough to recover.

Tully is a spectacular pocket meadow with great grazing for the stock though the meadow was pretty boggy in most spots. It was less than one half mile from a similar meadow called Horse Heaven. The camp was hidden in a little dry saddle in the pines. There was a tiny stream there which was the first place I ever saw in the sierra which had Lewis Monkeyflower, a tall mimulus that was bright yellow on the outside edges of the blossoms and bright pink inside.

While there I treated all of us to one of my more embarrassing moments. While mixing up some chocolate pudding for dessert, I was running off at the mouth about another trip long ago and far away where I had served that same dessert. Of course, instant pudding is not exactly the most delicious dessert in the world, but I'm not real fond of having guests tell me that. On the earlier trip a Marine on the trip took it on himself to be real insulting about it. I suggested that he shut up if he didn't want to wear some of the stuff. He handed out one last insult and took off running. With the best shot of my life I nailed him dead-center in the back with a huge spoonful of the stuff. He was probably thirty feet away when I got him. At this point in my bragging James bet me that I couldn't repeat the feat in question, walked about fifteen feet out on the meadow, faced me and hollered that I couldn't hit him even at that distance. Never good at knowing when to back off, I nailed him right in the chest. It wasn't a great loss of food as almost no one eats that stuff anyway. But it was a major loss of face as he gave a great yell, ran at me, and gave me a huge chocolate hug. Had to go take a bath and change my clothes. I'm pretty sure that that was the last time I used pudding as a weapon.

As I mentioned, the next day was our first layover day. We got to wash a week's worth of our laundry and Abigail got to rest over from her bout of colic.

Our next move was over Silver Pass, down to Pocket Meadow and on to Quail Meadow for our first resupply day. On this trip such a day was our first chance to receive our resupply of fresh food and horse grain to feed us all for the next seven days. Also, it was a chance send our trash and mail out with the resupply packer. This trip was so long that it became the first and only time I actually wrote weekly letters to my husband, LeRoy, while I was gone. I had visions of getting them back later to keep as a record of this great, long trip. Unfortunately, later when I asked for them he said, "Why would I keep those? I just threw them away." Guess my writing wasn't any more memorable then than it is now.

Actually, Tim, our resupply packer, arrived at our Quail Meadow camp just about the same time we did. That evening and the following morning were fairly chaotic as we sorted all our used stuff and garbage to go out and repacked all the new supplies and fresh food to go on south with us.

The next morning, we continued south on the John Muir Trail, crossing the bridge over Mono Creek and climbing over Bear Ridge. No real problems except that the boardwalk across the swampy area between the bridge and the base of the ridge had suffered some storm damage over the last winter. It had lost two or three 2x12 boards which meant that you were about four feet in the air, came around a corner, and discovered a big hole in your walkway. Getting your riding horse to jump it was pretty simple. Getting a string 1200 to 1500 pound mules carrying their big new loads to all jump that big ol' hole was pretty exciting, but Phil and his team of long ears made it. Then we started up the million or so switchbacks up Bear Ridge. Sometimes that trail section is blocked by down trees that the packer has to saw in half. Other times there have been big, active ground-wasp nests near the top. This time we were lucky enough to encounter neither. Without any further problems we came safely to our night camp on Bear Creek.

On that long climb I found myself pondering how our guests were adjusting to traveling for so long in such a small group. Pauline was simply enjoying her last trip in the "high lonesome". With James to take care of her, carry her duffle, and set up her tent she was doing fine. She had always needed the use of a narrow-bodied horse to help her cope with the hip surgeries she had had. This year she was riding Lolly, a nice narrow mule. She was one of the best of mules with the exception of the fact that she firmly believed that her rider owed her lots and lots of grass, flowers, weeds and all other possible munchies. In fact, Lyn teased Pauline about her animal's insatiable appetite.

When James wasn't looking out for his mom, he became interested in the skills of being a packer. First, he was catching, leading, and holding mules. Then he was helping Phil with the lifting and carrying of mule loads. Eventually he was packing mules, tying loads, and leading his own small string. By the end of the first week, he had become our second packer.

Lyn spent most of her time sharing her family scrapbook with the rest of us and taking pictures for the scrapbook she planned to make from this trip. Very sweet, kind lady. She and the other ladies often helped around camp, even calling themselves the PPP Patrol when taking down the privy before loading up to move in the morning.

The third lady guest on our trip was Diane. She was a frequent guest of Rock Creek Pack and had been on many different trips with us. She was good at taking care of herself on these trips. The only problem was that she was a non-stop talker. If you stayed still long enough for her to catch up with you, you were guaranteed to be treated to many long stories whether you wanted to or not. She especially liked to corner the guys so they would listen to her stories.

Our final guest was David Young. Well. He wasn't young at all in fact he was older than me. Despite that, he was an experienced and capable rider who knew his way around the high lonesome. He had injured his ankle prior to this trip, so he couldn't walk around very much. So most of the time he was on horseback, around the campfire, or in his tent. Diane often picked him as a conversational target. He stood it as long as he could then he would hobble away from camp or hide in his tent. Poor guy.

Despite all these little flukes including their being saddled with a grouchy old cook, we managed to work our way through the first fourteen days of this trip fairly easily.

With little real trouble we made our way to Bear Creek, up over Rosemarie Meadow, over Selden Pass and south into Kings Canyon. Then we climbed out of that canyon into Evolution Meadow and camped at Colby Meadow where James, who back home was a fan of bonsai plants, found a slick rock hillside covered in miniature twisted pine trees that looked a lot like nature's version of bonsai. When we left from there, we climbed over Muir Pass, getting a chance to visit the rock shelter on the very summit. Then we dropped into Le Conte canyon where we knew we could count on having a good campsite reserved for stock parties. It was in Little Pete Meadow and as we reached that area, it was starting to rain. Unfortunately, when we got there we found the stock site occupied by a single back packer. It was a camp large enough for seven people and fourteen head of stock, but this guy had his camp all set up and apparently didn't understand the sign that said "This site reserved for stock parties".

Mountain manners dictate that you can't just throw the guy out, so we searched around until we found an almost doable site high on the hillside. We managed to squeeze in a kitchen, a campfire, and room for a rain tarp. Our guests were wandering around trying to find room for their individual tents. Between the kitchen, a lot of manzanita and trees, a privy, and the picket lines for the livestock, they were having a pretty hard time. After a while, I was surprised to see the man who had swiped the stock camp, walking up to our camp. Though I'm pretty sure that he never really realized that he was in the wrong camp, he came by and said that he noticed that we were having trouble finding enough campsites. He said that he noticed that his camp was really way too big for one back packer and asked if any of our folks would like to move their tents down to share his big campsite. Without a moment's hesitation several of our guests moved down the hill to join the thoughtful back packer.

It was fortunate that they did as our kitchen ended up with wet blue jeans hanging, drying on the tarp ropes near the kitchen fires. Got a little tight. At least the rain stopped before it was too late and we pretty much made it through the night.

The next day we moved up to a small camp at the base of the "Golden Staircase" and the day after that we climbed up the staircase to the Palisades, across them and over Mather Pass. At the base of Mather Pass we stopped for late lunch and waited for our pack strings to catch up with us. We waited so long that Lyn got a picture of Pauline sound asleep on the tundra still holding Lolly's reins in her hand.

Well, we waited a long, long time. From the spot where we were waiting you could see the entire south face of the pass. That meant we should be able to see the packers coming a good hour before they got to us. As the afternoon wore on I started to worry. I had the guests, the horses, and a few small things in my saddle bags. The packers had all the food, shelter, clothes, and beds. I started figuring how to make it through the night if something dreadful had happened to out packers and supplies. The best things I had were matches and a good knife. Without going into too much detail, we finally saw them coming and made it to camp before it was too late. I asked Phil what had happened and he said that he had tied Topaz to a dead tree which turned out to be filled with a bee hive. The bees came after them causing a major wreck which took hours to rectify.

That night we finally camped above the trail to Taboose Pass. This was the 13th day of the trip. Tomorrow would be the last day for the first half of the trip. On the 14th day Phil, Pauline, James, Lyn, and Diane would pack up and leave the Sierra by way of Taboose Pass. Taboose is a pretty nasty pass and a long way down to the floor of the Owens Valley. Dave and I would remain in camp where we would soon be joined by our new packer, Jim Brumfield, and our two new guests. Jim would also be bringing a fresh string of mules and our second resupply of food and supplies for the remaining ten days of the trip.

One strange story that springs to mind at this point is one of those "pack cook" things. This whole menu had been planned to deal with the great length and constant movement of this trip. Besides the previously mentioned menu with its lack of repeats, seldom used new dishes, and lack of slow-cooking roasts and stews, I also couldn't keep any leftovers to be reused. The funny thing is that for unknown reasons, the only item that I actually saved as leftovers was a large jar of spaghetti sauce. On this morning as I was pulling out any food that had gone bad and should be sent out with the garbage, I discovered the sauce. When I tried to open it to see if it was still any good, it exploded in my hands. Guess it wasn't something I should have kept. It took some time to clean it all up and add it to the garbage. It was also fortunate that Dave and I would be spending most of the day hanging around camp. I knew the clothes I was wearing would require some scrubbing to remove the spaghetti sauce. That camp was also a great spot to look for arrowheads as it was on an ancient Indian trail across the sierra to the central valley. Apparently, Paiutes from the Eastern Sierra met members of the tribes from the west to trade obsidian from the Mammoth area for sea salt. Watching our horses and cleaning up camp also kept us busy until our new trail partners arrived late in the afternoon.

At this point, we got a new packer. Jim Brumfield was one of the absolute best packers anywhere in the Sierra. Dr. London had sent him on the southern end of this trip because he was one of the very few remaining packers who knew his way through the section of these mountains from Taboose to Crabtree. This included the two highest passes on the JMT, campsites that the Park Service would allow us to use, and areas where we could allow the stock to graze. Jim's other advantages were that he worked faster in camp than almost any other packer I had ever worked with. Also, he knew almost all the Park Service regulations and carried the rule book with him. Then of course he was a great storyteller around the campfire, and sang and played the guitar.

We also had two new guests who had survived their first day in over Taboose which is definitely a challenging pass. One of them was a thirtyish guy named Dave. Since we already had a Dave Young, we called the new guy Young Dave. It seems his area of expertise was computers. Our other guest was a tall guy about my age. For the life of me I can't remember his name, but he was tall, serious and an attorney for a major petroleum company. Though the new guys may have hoped for a rest, the next day began with us hitting the John Muir Trail southbound around Bench Lake. We then skirted around a number of smaller lakes and climbed up to Pinchot Pass. Pinchot Pass is one of the less terrifying passes in this part of the sierra, but the view off the summit certainly looks like it might be a long way down. Every time I rode there I was reminded of an earlier trip when a guest announced, "I know why it's called Pinchot. The second I looked off this thing my sphincter muscle went 'PINCHOT!!'" This trip gave me an opportunity to tell that joke again.

After the summit, the trail swung around to the northeast giving us a chance to miss the steepest part of the grade. Eventually the trail swung back around taking us down the easiest part of the slope. From this point we kept downhill past the trail to Woods Lake and Sawmill Pass. At this point I had a sudden memory of once meeting a Park Ranger cutting across the trail. He was more excited than any ranger I had ever seen. He had cut across country from the summit to the point where we met him. And along the way he had seen a wolverine. Since that was about 200 miles south of the nearest such siting, I was pretty excited, too.

We continued down trail past the turn off until we were at the old trail crew camp just below the 10,000-foot level. We were all pretty ready to camp for the night. The next few days we moved farther downstream then turned up another canyon toward Glen Pass. We camped down along the stream before climbing Glen the next day. It's a steep climb with a crest at 12,000 feet that consists of a thirty-foot-long window followed by numerous long switchbacks all the way down to Vidette Meadow. After a night at Vidette we started up the legendary Forester Pass. It's the highest pass on the John Muir at 13,200 feet and is guaranteed to scare the shit out of everyone. When I first came to work in the packing game many years ago, Charles Morgan described several of the worst passes to me and I swore I would never do Forester. This would be the second time for me to break that promise and very likely the last time. What a bitch of a pass. We planned to all ride up the north side as it is the better side. Coming down the "God-forsaken" south side we would loose-herd the pack mules and most of the riding animals. I took the lead walking with my Abby mule and leading the bell mare, Lopy. The only person actually riding was Dave Young who was either awfully brave or crazy as a hooty bird. Actually, he was too crippled up to walk. When we first got up to the top, Jim got off his horse and hunkered down by the pass sign. Then he threw me a disposable camera and told me to take his picture. Since I would have rather died, I threw the camera back at him and yelled at him to get us the hell off this thing. Heights scared me but looking at the 1200 feet of open air directly under his spurs pretty much freaked me out. Jim threw the camera to a passing backpacker and got his picture. Later he used it on the back cover of a book he wrote called, "Across the High Lonesome."

At this point I bailed off my mule and started leading down the first set of short, tight, narrow switchbacks. This whole set hung out over a sheer drop of 1200 feet. The only thing that impressed me was that I didn't pee my jeans. Then we swung in and crossed a coulee and then worked our way along a trail that was blasted in the side of the cliff. It felt a lot like going down a tunnel with one wall missing. Then we finally came out on a series of long switchbacks through jumbled talus, a lot more like all the other John Muir passes. After a while, Lopy decided it would be more fun to go first so she cut a switchback. Then I had to cut one to get ahead of her. So we finally reached the bottom with me in the lead, then Lopy, Abby, and a bunch of loose pack mules. On some of these truly terrifying passes, there is nothing as wonderful as getting close enough to the bottom that you can stop and tie your strings back together. You aren't exactly on the flat, but it feels close enough. Headed out across the alpine tundra felt absolutely lovely. It was quite a ways to that nights' camp on Tyndall Creek but I loved every step of it. It was such a relief that I never dreamed that our next few days would be an absolute nightmare. All I knew was that the next day would be our last layover day, and the day after that I would finally cross Bighorn Plateau, my last missing piece on the JMT.

Eventually we passed the ranger station at the head of Tyndall Creek. We went on down creek a couples of miles or so. We camped by the recently renovated "sheepherder's cabin." It was an interesting old log cabin with a roof made of dirt and rocks. I set up a cook fire, set up a kitchen tarp and got to work on dinner. It was cold and windy so Jim built a campfire down in a little pit. Before too long the park ranger showed up and without so much as a hello, he went to berating us for having two fires. He demanded that we put one out and the offered to ticket us for having two in the first place. He and Jim got into a pretty nasty argument. Then Jim went and got out all his books of park rules and demanded that the ranger show him where it said that. After a few more growls and nasty looks, the ranger headed back to his cabin offering to see Jim again tomorrow. Oh, well the next day was a layover and hopefully they could work it out. Little did I know that that was the least of our problems. You see, tomorrow was 9-11-2001. Yeah, that 9-11.

So, the next morning was a bit grey and looked like a storm might be moving in. Since none of us were watching TV, we had no idea what was going on in the rest of the world. We had breakfast and then did laundry early in hopes it might dry before the weather got worse. Sometime during the day Jim rode up to the ranger cabin to apologize. Along the way he met the ranger walking down the trail, apparently also to apologize. So that turned out well. Dave and I got a chance to saddle up and ride around the meadow. Jim got some pictures of us riding and hanging around the sheepherder cabin. The storm came on in around dinner time, I set up my bedroll under the kitchen tarp and Jim moved into the old cabin. By the time I went to bed it was snowing. I remember drifting off to sleep watching it fall.

The next thing I knew someone was shaking my bedroll and yelling at me. I woke up and realized that Jim was shaking his little AM radio in my face and yelling at me to listen to it. I sat up and asked him what the hell he was doing. By then it was most likely midnight in New York but the radio was still telling the whole story. Jim asked me if I thought it was real. I allowed as how I thought it was. We listened a while longer then discussed whether or not we should tell our guests. All three of our guests were what you could describe as solid and we decided that not telling them would be an insult. The next morning over coffee we told them what little we knew.

Soon we were on the trail just like any morning. Before long we were crossing the Bighorn Plateau, but it didn't seem to make much difference. Seemed like a potential "end of the world" was more important the finally finishing the Muir Trail. We were southbound on the JMT headed for Hidden Camp behind Crabtree Meadows and below Mt. Whitney. One creepy thing was that we didn't hear any airplanes. The Sierra are right along the passenger air routes connecting LA, Las Vegas, San Francisco, Reno, and Sacramento. Passenger jets traveling at 30,000 feet are always there. But not that week. It was completely quiet. A ways down the trail where Wright Creek crosses the JMT we came across a single hiker. She was sitting on a rock soaking her feet in the creek. She looked up and quietly asked me if I knew. I just gave a nod. I realized from her uniform that she was the head back country ranger for this section of the Kings Canyon-Sequoia Park. She looked up again and quietly asked if we had told our guests. I just nodded again. I told her where we were camping in case she needed to contact us and then we rode on. Later we found Hidden Camp and settled in. During the late afternoon we were enjoying the quiet of no planes and no hikers. Suddenly the thudding of helicopter blades shattered the silence and a small turquoise chopper suddenly popped into the air just above the trees on the edge of camp. It scooted over camp and up the hill headed right for the top of Whitney. It disappeared over the mountain and we assumed it was some kind of rescue. About a half hour later it popped up again and scooted over the trees in the direction it had come from. The remainder of that evening proved to be the only exception to the "no leftovers rule." The dinner itself was okay, but dessert was a magnificent English trifle. The guys ate until I thought they would explode. Later when I was cleaning up and went to throw it away, they defended it at knife point. And I finally agreed to save it if they promised to finish it off for breakfast, which they did.

The next day we moved to Nathan Meadow on Rock Creek. It was a short move and Jim entertained by singing and playing guitar late into the night. Our next day was our very last move. Over Siberian Pass, over the southern boundary of Sequoia Park, and over Cottonwood Pass to Horseshoe Meadow which was the end of our 24-day trip. The only evidence of the outside world was still the total lack of air traffic. Going down Cottonwood we met a backpacker actually running up the pass headed for the backcountry. He was carrying a huge pack and running up the steep part of the pass. He stopped long enough to shout that the world was coming to an end and he intended to die in the back country he loved.

So, we ended our trip at Horseshoe Meadows as we intended. And then unfortunately we had to return to the real world which was kind of a mess at that time. The nice part is that after 3 ½ weeks on the trail I was at home where I would find waiting for me one very fine husband, a dozen horses and mules, and half a dozen dogs. It was also the very first fall in thirty years where I didn't have to rush back to school to teach. Before I forget, I have three little bits to mention here.

1. Poor Pauline and James, who had left our trip at Taboose, finished their journey by going to San Francisco to spend a week with other old packing buddies who lived there. On 9-11-01 they had had enough visit and were boarding a flight to London when the whole airport shut down. They got to spend another week or maybe more before they could get transport home. Pauline wrote me a letter that even the best friend could get to be a bit of a burden.

2. My second note of interest comes from the Crabtree ranger I met the next year. He told me the rest of the story on the helicopter. First off, it was a rescue. There was a guy on top of Whitney with a broken arm. It was a compound fracture with bone sticking out of his upper arm. They couldn't get the bleeding stopped and were afraid he would bleed out. They had radioed up through the chain of command in the Park Service for permission to put a rescue ship in the air. The Air Force gave them special permission and sent that info down the chain of command to the fighter jets guarding the central valley. Unfortunately, someone dropped the ball and when the little turquoise helicopter popped out of the trees on his way to the hospital in Fresno, he found a fighter jet on either side of him with both pilots with their thumbs on the triggers. Fortunately, someone took command and called the fighters off. I guess it was a really close thing but everyone survived including the guy being rescued.

3. Remember earlier in this story where I couldn't remember the name of the third man on the last part of the trip. He was a memorable older, gentleman who was an attorney for a major oil company. After I finished writing this whole book, I suddenly remembered his name. Believe it or not, it was John Alden. Can you imagine being unable to remember such a name?

SAGE FLATS, MONACHE, AND BEYOND

In the Southern Sierra, the crest of the mountains makes a real change. Once you get south of Rock Creek, you leave the areas that were so heavily glaciated during the past ice ages. The mountain spires, U shaped canyons, hanging canyons, lateral moraines, glacial polish, and lakes all disappear. You discover that you are traveling on rounded hills and sandy meadows. The creeks meander instead of crashing down waterfalls. The only rough stuff seems to be volcanic cones and flows. Climbing up the eastern face of the sierras is pretty rugged, but once over the top you are on the Kern Plateau which is pretty easy going. The only mountains for miles seem to be Olancha Peak, Kern Peak, and Trail Peak which are easy enough that you could get stock up them if you had to.

Both in my early years with Mt Whitney Pack Trains and later when I was working for Rock Creek Pack Station, we worked this area when heavy snow years closed many of the trails farther to the north. It was easier country to travel, had good feed for the stock and great fishing for the guests. It even had some places where you could catch golden trout. Another entertainment for our guests who were cowboy wannabes was to watch the real thing work the cows and calves spending their summers on the Kern Plateau. The trail we took usually went over Summit, down to Monache, north through Brown, then Templeton, Ramshaw, Tunnel, Bullfrog, Mulkey, and out at Horseshoe. The cattle ranches working these areas were usually wintered in Owens Valley and included Anchor, Kemp, Brown, Cabin Bar, and Hunter.

Sometimes when we'd run across people working cattle up there, I would get an invitation to ride with them. This happened once at Little Whitney when the Thornberg girls were moving 200 pairs from that meadow up to Volcano Meadow the next day. It was a layover and my boss who was along said okay. It was a lot of fun and I learned two things. The first involves the fact that we were drinking beer and half-empty beer cans make a little krink noise that scared the hell out of my mule. She ran away with me but she was so slow that it didn't matter. The second was that if you have a guest who is a jerk who wanted to go but didn't get invited, he will stay mad at you for the whole rest of the trip. Often, I only got invited because in the outside world I was the hands' school teacher.

Herb London sent me on a lot of the southern trips simply because I was the only person working for Rock Creek that knew their way around that piece of country. On one trip that started out of Sage Flat and ended at Horseshoe Meadow we were joined by a dog. He was a nice little heeler and we figured he must have belonged to one of the ranchers at Sage Flat. After we left on the trip, we figured he would go home, but that night at Summit there he was. I figured that as we got farther from Sage Flat he would give up and go home. But every day he traveled with us and slept on my bed every night. We named him Sage and he stayed with us the whole way. There was no question that he was part of the crew. He traveled behind the string when we moved. When we were in camp, he would pick out a guest and join them in their activity. I saw him helping a fisherman, observing with a birder, and showing one lady where the evening primroses grew. At Ramshaw he even went with them to find the beaver dam. Every evening he sat by the campfire with the guests though I must admit he didn't have his own chair. A number of the guests wanted to adopt him and take him home after the trip. He was a great little dog and I would have loved to keep him. I got on my high horse insisting that Sage needed to be returned to his owner when we returned to front country. Finally, I talked to Jodi Olsen who lived in Lone Pine and Monache and knew everyone. She told me where Sage's owner lived. Two of my guests that were headed back toward LA agreed to make sure he got back to his owner. Sure wished I could have kept him. But fair is fair.

Yeah, fair is fair. At least that's what I thought until that fall. Jodi sent me a message that Sage's owner got tired of him running off so he shot him and killed him. Really blew me away. For a long time, I got really negative and wouldn't deal with anybody unless I could treat them bad. Didn't like myself much but there didn't seem to be much point in treating people fairly. Then one day driving passed the Rodeo grounds in town where they were roping, I saw Jodi. She waved me down and led me over to her truck. She said she wanted to show me something. In the back of her truck was a cute little heeler. Broke my heart. He looked just like Sage. She pointed and said, "Sage." I said, "Yeah, he looks just like him." She said, "No, you don't understand. This IS Sage!" Apparently, his owner had shot another dog and when Jodi found Sage, she just loaded him up, took him home, and kept him. She's obviously way smarter than I am. But I was pretty happy about it.